What is the Bahá'í Faith?

What is
the Bahá'í Faith?

An Introduction
for Young People

by

René Derkse

Translated from Dutch
by Olive McKinley

GEORGE RONALD

OXFORD

GEORGE RONALD, Publisher
46 High Street, Kidlington, Oxford OX5 2DN

Original Dutch edition
Het Bahá'í Geloof
© René Derkse 1983
This translation © George Ronald 1987

British Library Cataloguing in Publication Data

Derkse, René
  What is the Bahá'í faith? : an introduction
  for young people.
  1. Bahai Faith
  I. Title   II. Het Bahá'í geloof. *English*
  297'.89   BP365

  ISBN 0–85398–257–0

Phototypeset by Photoprint, Torquay, Devon
Printed and bound in Great Britain by
Richard Clay Ltd, Bungay, Suffolk

CONTENTS

CONTENTS

Preface

In writing this book I have tried to give you a clear outline of the teachings and history of the Bahá'í Faith. I do not know whether you know quite a lot about it already or whether you know a little, or even if you have only just heard the name 'Bahá'í' for the first time. So I have assumed that you know nothing about the Bahá'í Faith except its name.

I hope this book will be helpful to those who want to know what the Bahá'í Faith is about, and also to those who want to give a talk or write an essay about it.

Wishing you happy hours of reading.

René Derkse
Molenhoek, Holland

I
GOD AND HIS PROPHETS

1

The existence of God

Nowadays you meet quite a few people who say they do not believe in God. But you can only say 'I don't believe in that' if you know what it is that you do not believe in. In other words, you first have to form an idea of the thing, and then you can say whether or not you believe in it.

For instance, if I say that I do not believe the earth is round, then I must at least have my own idea of what a round world would be like. So if someone says he does not believe in God, he must have some idea, some image of God. Maybe he is thinking of an old man with a long beard, seated on a throne up in Heaven. It is not surprising that a person who thinks like this does not believe in God. I do not believe in that idea of God either and I doubt whether anyone does now. Yet not so long ago many people thought of God like that. But now that we know what is above the clouds and what the universe looks like, we can no longer accept that God sits up there on a throne.

And yet the strange thing is that those people who do not believe in God can sometimes be heard to say: 'There must be something. I don't know what it is but there must be something.' Perhaps you have thought this yourself sometimes. And do you know when people usually say this kind of thing? When they see something they cannot explain or cannot understand.

Just think of the birth of a child. This is something everyone finds difficult to understand. It seems miraculous that an object as tiny as a fertilised egg can grow into something so tremendous. You will often hear people saying: 'Isn't it wonderful how you suddenly have a complete human being that can see and hear, with its own tiny heart and lungs, and that can move its arms and legs? Oh, there must be something, there must be something . . .'

Now we all know that a baby cannot make itself: that is impossible. And we all know, too, that we could never make a human being ourselves. Some scientists are able to make a robot, but not a person with a will of his own, an individual character and personal opinions. It cannot be done. So who made the baby, then?

It is obvious that everything which exists, that you can see, is made by someone. Whether it be a house, a racecourse or a poster. Something you can see must have been made by someone. So a baby must have been made by someone or by some creative force.

Take an artificial flower. You know it was made in a factory somewhere. But a real flower is much more beautiful, isn't it? A real flower smells sweetly and is a growing thing unlike an artificial flower. Yet we do not know of anyone who can make a flower that grows. But you cannot therefore say that the real flower has not been made or created. Of course it has been made. The point is that it was made by something we cannot see or hear or feel or taste or smell.

We cannot perceive this creative force with any of our five senses: not with our eyes or ears, tongues or noses or by touching it. We say that this creative force is not perceptible to the senses. But that does not mean it does not exist.

And if you are thinking about something, your thoughts cannot be perceived by the senses. But the thoughts are there, going through your head. So if you tell me you have an idea, I believe it even though I cannot see it.

And so it is, too, with the creative force. Although I cannot perceive it with the senses, still I know it is there, because I can see the results. For example, I can see how a plant comes up from the earth and keeps growing bigger. I can also see the result of your thought when you put away your geography book, for instance, and pick up a comic.

Now there are people who will say: 'Listen, that plant is growing because it is getting rain and sunlight. It has nothing to do with any creative force.'

Do you know what I ask people like that? I ask them where the sun gets its power from. And anyway, where does the sun itself come from? Because it is true, is it not, that the sun has not always been there? It must somehow have come into existence. It must have had a beginning. For everything made has a beginning, whether it is a car, a cassette, a tree, an animal or a human being. And so there must be something which made the sun and gave it power, and gave the rainwater the power to make the plant grow. And something that made the fertilised egg grow into a perfect child who can see and hear and think and feel and move.

And that 'something' is a creative force which has power over all created things: the sun, stars and the whole universe; over every living thing: plants, animals, human beings, your own heart which keeps on beating. And so we call that 'something' the Almighty, the Powerful, the Creator or God. And although we cannot perceive this God with our senses, we can still believe in Him.

Now you may not like this word 'God' since it reminds you of that wise old man who lives in Heaven. But that does not mean you can no longer use that word. If I think Mary is an actress and find out later that she is a singer, I do not go around saying she is not to be called Mary any more. What I have to change is the image I have of Mary. In the same way we must change our ideas about God, but not His name.

2

God's purpose

In Chapter 1 we came to the conclusion that a creative force exists. From now on we shall call this force God. We have also seen that God has created an enormous number of things and continues to do so. Every year new plants grow, young animals are born and new people come into the world. In fact, it would be true to say that everything is created by God, including mankind.

In this chapter and those to follow we shall no longer consider plants or animals, but ourselves: Man. Now, God did not create man just for fun, but for a particular purpose. Which is quite logical, of course. You only have to look at the world around you. A sweets manufacturer makes his product for the purpose of selling it to you or someone else to enjoy. And I have written this book so that you and other young people can read it. And if you make a picture in your spare time, you do so for a particular purpose. Perhaps you want to give it to someone, or hang it on the wall in your own room. So you see, when someone makes something, it is done for a purpose. In the same way God created man for a particular purpose.

Now that we have realised this, you may be interested to know for what purpose God created you and me. But if we want an answer to this question we are going to meet with one big problem. Let me explain.

In the first chapter I said that God cannot be perceived with the senses. That means, therefore, that we cannot see or hear God. And that is a difficulty, for how are we to discover what God wants of us? How can we get to know God? Let me put the question in another way: how can I get to know a person who exists but whom I can never see or hear? If you think about this, you will see there is only one way. I can only get to know that person through someone else who knows the person very well. For example, a friend.

Now in our case it is God Who wants us to know Him and in this way to find out the purpose for which He created us. And since God knows that we cannot perceive Him with our senses, He therefore sends someone into the world from time to time who does know Him and who knows exactly what God wants of us. Such a Person is called a Prophet or Manifestation of God. God manifests Himself (which means that God makes known His will and His purpose to mankind) through His Prophet. And because the Prophet or Manifestation of God is able to 'hear God's voice', He has a very special place in creation. He occupies a position, as it were, between God and Man. This means, therefore, that if we want to get to know God we must turn to His Manifestation, His Prophet. However, before we take a look at what God has said to us through His Prophets, we shall examine in the next chapter why it is necessary for us to know God and to know what His will is.

3

The need for a Manifestation

We now know that God makes known His will, that He
reveals it to mankind through a Prophet or Manifestation.

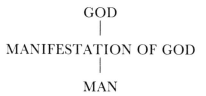

GOD
|
MANIFESTATION OF GOD
|
MAN

You could also regard such a Manifestation as the Mouth-
piece of God; God speaks to man through Him. You could
also call Him a Messenger. After all, He brings a message
from God to man. And God sends us that message because
He wants us to be happy people, living in the world at
peace with one another.

Now, I daresay that if I asked you whether you wanted to
be happy, you would immediately say 'Yes'. In fact, I could
ask everyone the same question and they would all give the
same answer: 'Yes, I do.' And yet, if you look around you,
there are very few people who are happy. There is always a
war somewhere or people are hurting one another.

But why? Everyone wants to live in peace and yet all the time they fail. There have been so many people who have said: 'If we do this or that, we shall be happy'. But we are still not happy. After the Second World War a number of people set up the United Nations to ensure that there would never be war again. And yet, to this very day, wars keep breaking out. Why is this? Everyone wants to be happy and all make plans to be happy, and yet they cannot manage to live together in peace.

To give you a better understanding of how this comes about, let me give you another example. Suppose you and your friends want to learn to play the guitar. Together you plan how you will do it. You buy a guitar and start playing it. You discover a way which you think is the best. One of your friends disagrees and says he knows a better way. Yet another says both of you are wrong and will never learn the guitar that way. However, by the end of a year not one of you can play the guitar properly. And at the end of the second year you still cannot. All you do is argue about the proper way to play.

Adults do the same thing. For instance, none of them wants a nuclear war but they keep arguing about how to prevent it. One person thinks that both America and Russia should reduce their nuclear armaments. Another thinks that America should set an example and first abolish its own nuclear weapons. Yet another feels that the Americans should have more nuclear arms than the Russians because then the latter will not dare to start a nuclear war. And all these people think their own plan is the best and that the others are no good. But how do you know who is right? Perhaps no one is right and there is yet a better way to rid the world of war. The problem is, how can you find out?

Let's go back to the guitar. You and your friends all want to be good players and have made all kinds of plans for this, yet you have not succeeded. Why is this? It is because you have never got hold of anyone who knows all about playing the guitar, such as a teacher or a first-class guitarist who can play anything, be it jazz, rock or classical music. He is familiar with every style and every problem. That is why only he can tell you the best way to learn to play. Only he can solve your problems and put an end to your arguments.

So, just as with the guitar, you will have to find someone who knows all about mankind and can show us exactly how to get out of our difficulties, and how to live in peace together. And who do you think would know mankind best? I will ask the question in another way: who knows most about my car? Who knows exactly how it is put together and what needs to be done if it gives any trouble? The answer is obvious. It is the maker of the car.

So if we ask ourselves who knows exactly how human beings are made, how they function, think and act, what they can do and what they cannot, and what is best for them, the logical answer must be: the one who made or created them. And that is the Creator, or God. And since we now know that God has revealed Himself through His Manifestations, we also know that if we want peace we will have to listen to whatever the Manifestation or Messenger of God has to say to us. Only He can be our teacher since He alone knows mankind through and through and can say exactly what is best for us. Only He knows what we must do to live peacefully together.

But then we must naturally listen carefully to what He says and really try to do what He tells us. Otherwise we shall fail again. If you only listen to what your guitar teacher says but do not try to do it, you will naturally never be a good player.

In short, we now know that God knows us best and that, if we want to be happy together, we must listen to His teachings. We also know that He has given His teachings to us through His Manifestations or Messengers. And finally we also realise how important it is to do what He teaches us. Otherwise we still won't be the happy people that we want to be.

4

The Manifestations of God

In this chapter we shall take a closer look at what a Manifestation of God is and what Manifestations there have already been. In the previous chapter we came to the conclusion that the Prophet is, first and foremost, a divine Teacher who can show us the only right way to happiness and peace.

Since we have seen that no man has ever been able to do this, we cannot say that a Manifestation of God is merely a very special kind of man. If He were, He could never show us the right way either. Moreover, He tells us what God wants to say to us. And since it is God who knows mankind best of all – for He created us Himself – His Manifestation also knows us better than any human being does. And therefore God's Messenger has a special place in creation; His station is higher than man's. He may have all the outward appearance of a human being, but spiritually, in His way of thinking and acting, He is not the same as we are. That would be impossible, since we need to learn about God through Him. If the Manifestation were only a special human being and therefore imperfect like everyone else, sometimes saying things which were incorrect, this would mean that God was also imperfect and sometimes said things which were incorrect. And of course that is not the case.

In addition, it is only reasonable that if the Messenger of God wishes to teach us to be honest, for example, He Himself must be completely honest. It also stands to reason that if someone wants to teach you how to acquire an excellent French accent, he himself must have a faultless French accent. This is why the Manifestation of God is perfect. Otherwise He could never give perfect teachings, a perfect education, to mankind.

But there is something else which shows that the Manifestation of God is not merely a very special human being. As you probably know, throughout history there have been great thinkers who sometimes had very fine ideas about life. And such thinkers began to attract followers who were in agreement with them. Yet the ideas or teachings of these thinkers usually had little influence on ordinary people. Usually, only those who were educated knew about their ideas. And after the passing of some decades, or even sooner, people began to have doubts about the truth of those teachings and another philosopher appeared who presented new ideas.

It is all quite different with the teachings brought by the Messengers of God. They received hardly any help or support from other people. They were all alone. And it was particularly the educated and powerful who rejected Their teachings, ridiculed Them and caused Them to be banished or put to death.

But in spite of this, Their teachings had an even stronger influence after Their deaths – an influence which lasted for hundreds, even thousands, of years. To this day you meet many people who are trying to live in accordance with the teachings of a Manifestation of God who died thousands of years ago. If you think about that for a moment, you may call it a miracle. Because not even a very special human being has ever been able to accomplish that.

Now that you have a clearer notion of what a Manifestation of God is, let us make the acquaintance of some of them. Before doing so, however, we should remember that there must have been many whose names are unknown to us because they belong to the distant past before history was recorded. There can never have been an age without guidance given by God through His chosen Messenger. Otherwise, God would be unjust to the people who lived in such a time.

So let us start with the best known of the early Manifestations: Noah. This Prophet tried to make people understand that there was indeed a God and why it was important to believe in Him. But the people only laughed at Noah and some even attacked Him violently. Others reproached Him or ridiculed Him. In spite of all this, Noah always remained kind, and He warned the people of a great flood which was soon to come upon them. When it came, anyone who was not willing to live according to the Will of God would perish. However, most people went on thinking that Noah's warning was just a lot of nonsense. Only a few began to believe in Noah and therefore again in God. What Noah had foretold actually happened: a tremendous flood swept over their country and all the people who had laughed at Noah and scoffed at God perished miserably.

Then, a few centuries later, Abraham appeared. He, too, was born at a time when the people had long forgotten the teachings of the previous Manifestation. In fact, His own people no longer believed in one God but in many. Abraham, however, refused to believe in all those gods because He knew that there was only one God. Those around Him would not accept this and even the members of His own family were so angry with Abraham that He had to leave the country of His birth. They thought that anyone who dared to insult their gods ought to be destroyed. But in spite of His banishment Abraham did not die as people had hoped. On the contrary, He was able to reach the Holy Land (now Israel), where, as time passed, He and His descendants prospered. God had promised to make Him 'father of many nations', and that is what He became through His descendants: Isaac, Ishmael, Moses, Christ and Muhammad. Through Them His teachings have indeed spread throughout the world.

The next Manifestation of God lived about 3,200 years ago. And now nearly everyone knows His name: He was called Moses. The religion connected with His name still exists today and still has millions of members. This is the Jewish religion – or Judaism – of which you have certainly heard. This in itself is quite extraordinary. Don't you think it is quite amazing that there are still so many people in this day and age who follow the teachings of someone who has been dead for over three thousand years? You begin to realise what a tremendous influence Moses must have had.

Even the wisest philosopher has never had such a strong and lasting effect on people.

But there is another marvellous thing about Moses. He managed, without using violence, to free a whole nation from slavery and bondage. Can you see an ordinary person achieving that? I can't. But Moses succeeded. He got His people out of Egypt and back to Israel, the Holy Land. It was Moses who made these people – whom a cruel Pharoah in Egypt had humiliated – very famous. It was He who turned them into the wisest nation of His time. He brought the 'children of Israel' to such a high level of development that even the philosophers of Greece came to the learned of Israel in order to increase their knowledge. If you take into account that Moses had been no more than a simple shepherd who could not even hold a proper conversation because He stuttered so badly, one thing becomes clear: Moses must have been helped by a divine power. He must have been a Manifestation of God.

Over one thousand years later we come across the name of the Manifestation of God that Westerners know best. This was Jesus Christ and, as you know, He too came from a humble background since His father was a simple carpenter. And He too came at a time when the people of Israel were being oppressed by another people. This time it was the Romans who dominated and despised the Jews. But, in spite of the fact that the coming of Christ had been foretold by all the Prophets, including Moses, hardly anyone believed in Him. The Jewish priests certainly did not. They even wanted to get rid of Jesus as quickly as possible.

And why was this? Christ had not done away with the Law of Moses but He was spreading a new religion which was not merely intended for the Jews but for all people. Which meant for the Romans too, the enemies of the Jews. In addition, the priests were all much too afraid that they would lose their own power if people began to follow Christ.

When Jesus indeed began to be popular, they condemned Him, saying He was a liar, and had Him crucified. And most of the Jews allowed themselves to be persuaded by the priests. In spite of this, after His death His teachings spread all over the world and one country after another came under the influence of His words, words which taught people to love their neighbours and be tolerant.

Approximately six hundred years later, in other words about 1400 years ago, another Messenger of God was born. His name will also be familiar to you. This was Muhammad, the Founder of Islam, a religion which has hundreds of millions of followers today. This Manifestation of God lived among the Arabs, who at that time were an exceedingly savage and cruel people. So savage, in fact, that one of their tribes had the custom of burying their new-born daughters alive, just because they were girls. And when these tribes went to war, the victors took all the women and children from the opposing tribe and treated them as slaves. In addition, a husband could treat his wives in whatever way he liked. He could kill one of them or keep her a prisoner in a pit. He could strike her, curse her or molest her. For he was her master and she had no say. Besides, these Arab tribes lived by plundering and stealing and so they were constantly engaged in fighting and making war. They killed each other, plundered and destroyed each other's possessions and captured women and children, whom they sold to strangers.

You can understand that the Arabs wanted nothing to do with Muhammad, who came to tell them that they must not kill or steal and that they must make friends with their enemies. Many of Muhammad's followers, therefore, were tortured and abused and driven out of their homes. These violent persecutions lasted for thirteen years. Then, in the middle of the night, Muhammad fled from the city of His birth to Medina. His followers also left and some even fled to other countries. However, their enemies simply carried on with their persecutions, even following Muhammad to Medina and some of His followers as far as Africa.

Only one course was left to Muhammad. He must protect, in whatever way He could, those who had come to believe in God and in Him. And this is the reason that Muhammad allowed the believers to defend themselves against the barbarians who had assembled large armies in order to kill Him and His followers. Not only did they fight their enemies but they were victorious, thus bringing the bloodshed to an end. The savage Arab tribes were so impressed by Muhammad's power that they began to believe in Him and in God. The tribes made peace with each other and the Arabs made such progress as a people that by the Middle Ages they had become the most civilised and learned nation in the world. Once again, someone who had never received any formal education had achieved unimaginable feats, feats which were only possible to some-

one who was aided by the power of God: a Manifestation of
God.

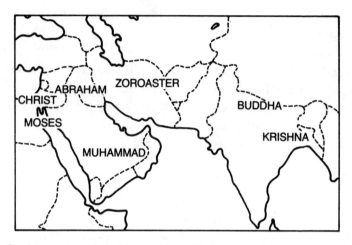

God has revealed Himself to all the peoples of the world.
We know, for instance, that about three thousand years ago
a Manifestation was also born in India. His name was
Krishna. He, too, taught His people about life and about
God. There have also been other Prophets, like Buddha,
Who was born about 2,500 years ago in the Himalayas and
Who became the Founder of Buddhism, a religion which
still has hundreds of millions of followers. In Persia, too,
another Messenger of God also lived some 2,500 years ago,
called Zoroaster. We also know that in America, a very
long time ago before any white people lived there, they had
their Prophets, although we do not know Their names now.

Of course this does not mean that a Manifestation of God
must have lived in every part of the world and neither was
this necessary. In fact, the sketch-map shows that the

Founders of all present-day world religions lived in the Middle East or India. But as we have seen, their influence was so great that their teachings spread to many lands. What we can be sure of is that God has provided for every human being to come into contact with the teachings of His Manifestations. And that is what matters!

*'The
foundations of
the religions
of God
are one
foundation.'*
— 'Abdu'l-Bahá

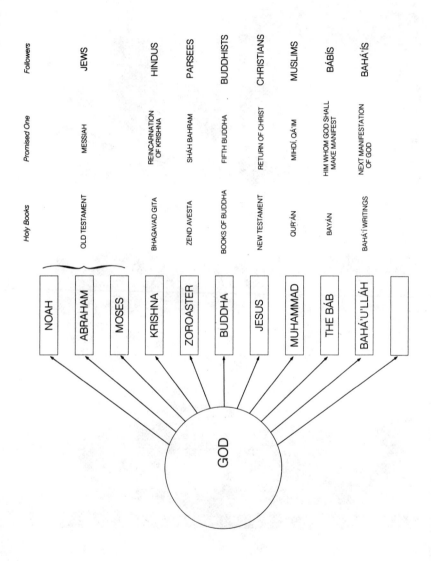

	Holy Books	Promised One	Followers
NOAH			
ABRAHAM	OLD TESTAMENT	MESSIAH	JEWS
MOSES			
KRISHNA	BHAGAVAD GITA	REINCARNATION OF KRISHNA	HINDUS
ZOROASTER	ZEND AVESTA	SHÁH BAHRAM	PARSEES
BUDDHA	BOOKS OF BUDDHA	FIFTH BUDDHA	BUDDHISTS
JESUS	NEW TESTAMENT	RETURN OF CHRIST	CHRISTIANS
MUHAMMAD	QUR'ÁN	MIHDÍ, QÁ'IM	MUSLIMS
THE BÁB	BAYÁN	HIM WHOM GOD SHALL MAKE MANIFEST	BÁBÍS
BAHÁ'U'LLÁH	BAHÁ'Í WRITINGS	NEXT MANIFESTATION OF GOD	BAHÁ'ÍS

GOD

5

The unity of God's Manifestations

Let us recap on a number of important points. We have seen that it is God Who knows Man best and therefore also knows best how to make him happy. For this purpose He sends His teachings, through His Manifestations, Who pass them on to us. If this is what happens, one cannot say that one Manifestation has spoken the truth and another Manifestation has not. So how can we say, for instance, that only Christ has brought the truth and no one else? If this were so, it would mean that there is not one God but just as many gods as there have been Prophets. And this is not true, since each Messenger, including Christ, has clearly stated that there is only one God. But if there is only one God, there is only one truth. This becomes quite clear if you compare the teachings of the Manifestations with each other. Then you see quite clearly that there are many more similarities than differences between these teachings. The Messengers of God have stated that we should try to be honest, just, tolerant and kind; that it is not good to be jealous, greedy, selfish, violent or discontented. In addition, the Prophets have made it clear to mankind that others too have brought a true message from God.

If anyone has the right to say that only Jesus Christ was a true Messenger of God, then a follower of Muhammad also has the right to claim that Muhammad was the only true Prophet. However, Muhammad in His time told the Muslims that they must accept Christ. In the Qur'án He stated clearly that the Christians and the Jews were under the protection of God. And that if a Muslim were to marry a Christian woman, he should not prevent her from going to church. And if the Christians wished to build a church, the Muslims should help them. In the same way, Jesus never rejected the teachings of Moses or turned His followers (the Jews) away.

So you see the Prophets themselves have never been the cause of disunity. It was their followers who were responsible for discord. After the deaths of their Manifestations, it was they who began to make war on the followers of other religions. Why did they do so? For no better reason than because they had begun to think that it was only their own Prophet Who had spoken the truth and that only their own religion was right.

Eventually, things get so bad that the followers of a particular religion are unable even to preserve unity within their own religion. This is why, only a few centuries ago, large numbers of people were killed or burned at the stake because they began to interpret the words of Christ in a different way. It even came about that two Popes were at war with each other. If you think about this, it is really very stupid and rather ridiculous. And did you know that fifty years ago, in some countries a Catholic child was not allowed to have a Protestant child as a friend? Even though they both believed in the same Jesus Christ. And did you know that if a Protestant man married a Catholic woman, people thought the Devil slept between them? It sounds incredible but it is quite true. And actually I think it is very sad because the Manifestations of God never wanted this. On the contrary, They have always taught mankind to be tolerant and to love everyone, even those who belong to other religions.

So there are really a great many similarities between the religions. But there are some differences too. Why is this?

In the first place we must remember that mankind has developed and progressed over the years. Just like a child who develops all the time until he or she reaches adulthood. Let us compare God with a father and mankind with a child. When you are bringing up a child you will, for example, teach him not to steal. As a father you forbid it. And it does not matter how old your child may be, whether he is four years old or ten, the command remains the same. We find this in religions too. It does not matter when the Prophet came, whether it was two thousand or six thousand years ago, He still forbids us to steal. This is one of the similarities between all religions.

But let us take another example. Your four-year-old brother wants to ride a bicycle to school. Because the way is across a busy street and he is too small to manage this, he will not be allowed to do so. But your brother grows older and the time comes when he is big enough to ride his bicycle to school and he is no longer forbidden to go on his own. You can see a clear difference here between what was at first forbidden and then allowed.

This can also be found in the religions. One Manifestation of God may forbid something while another allows it. This is because mankind, as it were, is getting 'older'. The Manifestations therefore change certain teachings because times have changed and mankind also changes.

Let me give you another example. Let us go back to the first class in the primary school. In this, the teacher tells you something about the human body. He does not tell you very much about it but it is enough for you. You do not need to know any more and, in any case, you would not understand if the teacher went into detail about the digestive system or some other part of the body. But now you are older. What would you think if your teacher told you exactly the same things as the teacher you had in your first class? You would not like it because now you can understand much more than you could then. You have lots of new questions that you want answered.

Well, the same thing is true of religion. Each time a Manifestation of God appears, He tells people just as much as they can understand. And since people are progressing all the time, they can understand more and so the Prophets tell them more. And they explain things slightly differently from the way in which the previous Manifestation had done. Just as a teacher explains the working of the heart in a different way to a six-year-old and to a twelve-year-old. With the younger child he must use quite different words and simpler explanations than when he is talking to a child of twelve.

But there is also another reason for the differences between religions. This is because one nation is different from another. Here again, the Messenger of God adapts His teachings, just as a good teacher adapts his lessons to his pupils. You know yourself that the way in which a teacher explains a mathematical problem to you does not always make it clear to you. He may explain it a hundred times in this way but you still won't understand it. One day, though, he tries again but this time in quite a different way. And what happens? Suddenly you have got it and you do not know why it seemed so difficult. The Manifestations do this too. They explain the same problem to one people in a different way than to another, for the simple reason that people are different.

To sum up: the Manifestations of God are in unity because They have all been sent by the same God. Their teachings are in essence the same. The differences depend on the amount of knowledge They have already revealed and the way in which They have explained it. And this is because the Messengers of God lived at different times and among different peoples. In addition, each nation has its own difficulties and each age its own problems, for which the Manifestation of God provides the solution.

6

The times in which we live

In talking about the various Manifestations of God we have seen that They all appeared among peoples who were living in troubled times. We have also seen that the Manifestations of God were able to help people to overcome their difficulties and set them on the road to progress. In this way, each religion has reached a high point of development and gone through a period when it flourished. Yet this has always come to an end, and each religion has fallen into decay. Gradually the feelings of love for God, for His Manifestation and for mankind have faded. And when love for someone has gone, you are not so inclined to do your best for that person.

This is why the believers are not so inclined to follow the teachings of their Prophet. It was all so long ago. And it is so difficult to like everyone, and to be sincere and willing to do things for others. It is really much easier to do what you want yourself. This is like the child who says he is going roller-skating on the main road no matter what, because it is much better there. The child who thinks he knows best does not obey his father and does what he likes. But such a child will get into trouble, and skating on the main road may even cost him his life.

And so people get into difficulties, too, because of their stubbornness. They make war, plunder and kill. They become dishonest and unfriendly and only engage in making things easier for themselves. Others are left to sort out their own problems. It is nothing to do with those living in comfort. But of course, because of the actions of yet others, these people get into difficulties themselves. Perhaps they are robbed or lose a child in war. And whose fault is that? Who is to blame? God, of course. He has allowed it all to happen. Even though the people themselves have turned aside from God. And if another Manifestation of God appears at a time like this, He is called a fool and no one wants to have anything to do with Him. That is how foolishly the people behave. Does this remind you of our own times? It does me. It makes me think of the First World War and of the Second, and of all the other wars that are going on at present. Then I think of all those accounts in the newspapers of robberies and murders.

Then on the street I see so many unfriendly faces and meet so many people who are afraid of the future. People who do not believe in God or His Manifestations. People who say that God is dead because He allows so much misery to happen in the world. Such people forget that they are not prepared to take the trouble to live in accordance with God's teachings.

Yes, this is indeed a time in which mankind badly needs a Manifestation of God. We do not seem to be able to solve our own problems. Only a divine Teacher can get us out of our difficulties. No one else.

Now there are some people who say that a new divine

Teacher is not necessary. According to these people, we just have to look at what Jesus Christ, Moses, Buddha or Muhammad taught. They forget that we now live in a completely different age. And that this age has quite different problems from those of one, two or three thousand years ago. In addition, they disagree about which Manifestation of God we ought to consult. The Christians naturally feel it should be Christ and the Buddhists that it should be Buddha, etc. As well as this, we find that every Christian has a slightly different interpretation of the words of Jesus, which is another cause of disagreement. It is therefore of no use to seek the solution to our problems from the divine Teachers of the past.

And it is not necessary either, since each Manifestation of God has promised us that a new Messenger of God will come in the future. Jesus promised His disciples, for example, that He would surely return to tell them those things which they could not yet understand. He did say, however, that He would then have a new name. He also urged them to be vigilant since He would return at a time when they did not expect Him. All the other Manifestations of God have promised Their followers that a time would come at which a new Messenger would appear. And according to all the Prophets, this would be One who would finally, after so many centuries of conflict, usher in a time of no more war or violence. A time in which all nations and races would form an alliance with one another and live together in peace.

In fact, all the Manifestations of God have told us what such a time will be like, the age in which the promised

Universal Teacher will come. Let us take a number of these descriptions and list them:

1. There will be wars and rumours of wars (Bible).
2. The Jews will return to the Holy Land, i.e. Israel (Bible).
3. The religions will be divided into sects and the sects will disagree (Bible).
4. People will be unjust (Bible, Islamic Traditions).
5. In those times people on one side of the world will be able to see people on the other side (Islamic Tradition); lamps will be lit without candles by merely touching the walls, carriages will be driven without horses and men will fly like birds (Zoroastrian prophecy).

Now, if we examine these descriptions it will be clear that they refer to our own times, because:

1. There are wars.
2. The Jews are back in Israel.
3. There is conflict between the religions (for example, the Christians and Muslims in Lebanon) and the sects (Northern Ireland, Iran and Iraq).
4. There is much injustice (for example, the extremes of wealth and poverty, racial prejudice and discrimination, lack of education, etc.).
5. We now have television, electric light, motor cars and aeroplanes.

All this can mean only one thing: the promised Universal Teacher, the new Manifestation of God, must have come. And this is really good news, for we need Him badly. We are up to our necks in trouble and have so many problems for which we cannot find solutions.

God, our Creator, foresaw this, however, and wanted to help us. This is why He has once again sent His guidance to us through His new Manifestation. He was born in Persia and lived from 1817 to 1892. His name was Bahá'u'lláh. This Arabic word means the Glory of God.

But alas, when this new Manifestation appeared, most people would have little or nothing to do with Him either. And most people still ignore Him. Many people still think that they do not need God or His Manifestation and that they can solve their own problems. And in spite of the fact that difficulties increase day by day, they still maintain that their own ideas are the best.

And yet at the present time there are followers of Bahá'u'lláh in 235 countries or dependent territories of the world. People who are working for a happier world and who believe that only our Creator can show us the right way to do this. People who realise how important are the teachings of Bahá'u'lláh and who are eager to pass them on to anyone who wants to hear about them. Just like the influence of Jesus Christ and of every other Manifestation of God, Bahá'u'lláh's influence cannot be held back, and a time of real happiness and peace will come.

II
THE TEACHINGS OF
BAHÁ'U'LLÁH

7

Teachings for the well-being of the world

You probably all know the saying, 'If you want to improve the world, start with yourself.' You may find this a bit of a cliché but that does not mean that the first person who said it was not right. In fact, if everyone remains the same, holding on to the same ideas, the world will stay as it is. And that would not be very desirable. So if we want to change the world, we shall have to be ready to change our own ideas first. This means that when we investigate something we do not start by saying, 'It isn't true anyway.' Or think, 'This book won't make any sense.'

Bahá'u'lláh teaches that if we want to investigate whether something is true or not, we must do so without prejudging it. It does not make sense to study the Bahá'í Faith if you are determined to believe that there is no God and that religion is nonsense. That is obvious.

Bahá'u'lláh also says that we should not imitate others, since as long as people go on accepting without question the opinions of others, even their parents, nothing will change. So if a person says he is a Catholic because his parents are Catholics, he is just imitating them. Blindly following the beliefs of others is not much use when it comes to changing the world. It is different if a person says, 'I chose to be a Catholic because I studied this religion and decided it was the best.' This person has investigated for himself and thought things out for himself. Bahá'u'lláh says that everyone should investigate truth independently and without prejudice. This also applies to the children of Bahá'í parents.

If we talk about improving the world, that must mean there is something wrong with it. In one way or another, life on our planet is not all that we would like it to be. The question is how can we improve it. To discover the answer we need to know what is wrong and why.

Let me give you an example. Imagine you are sick. You are in bed and would naturally like to be feeling better. Before you can get well, you need to know what is wrong with you. Let us say you have a dreadful stomach-ache. Now, I can give you a stomach tablet and the pain will certainly go away. But then what happens? Within a couple of weeks you have the pain again. I can give you another tablet but that will not help you much. The pain may soon be back. So what must I do? I must find out why you keep getting stomach-aches. What is causing them? If it turns out that you drink too much coffee and that this gives you the pain, then we can really solve your problem. You have got to stop drinking so much coffee.

Well, this is the way we need to approach the problems of mankind as a whole. First we must find out what is wrong. That is not too difficult, since we only need to look in the newspaper. There we will soon discover, for example, that there is war or violence or bloodshed of some kind going on somewhere every day. Now it is possible for some prominent person to try to talk to the opposing sides and get them to make peace. This sometimes happens. Usually, however, these talks do not succeed. There may be a lull in the shooting but it soon begins again and the war just goes on.

We might compare this with the stomach tablet. As long as we do not know the cause of the fighting, the call to peace (stomach tablet) will only stop it for a short time. So we first need to know the cause of the fighting. Which is more easily said than done, since so far no one has been able to find it or provide the right solution. In Chapter 3 I discussed the reasons for this. We also saw that the one who knows man best can only be the one who made him. In other words, God. Only God, therefore, through His Manifestation, can show us the way to happiness and peace. So it stands to reason that we should take a closer look at what Bahá'u'lláh says on this subject, since He is the most recent Manifestation of God.

When we investigate the teachings of Bahá'u'lláh we immediately notice that everything He says is centred on the unity of mankind. The achievement of this unity is the goal that God has set for modern man. That is His Will for the time in which we live. So if we wish for peace and well-being, we must first make efforts to be united. All our thoughts and actions should be directed towards this goal.

In this connection it is important to realise that every human being was created by one and the same God. Only through this knowledge can we begin to see and treat each other as equals. Only when we realise that everyone was created in the same way and came into existence through the same power, can we really feel unified. And this feeling is necessary if we want to achieve the unity of mankind.

Looking at the world around us, we see that we are a long way from such unity. In fact, what we see is often the greatest disunity. So it is important to study what Bahá'u'lláh says about the causes of war and discord. As we saw in Chapter 5, it was often the Prophet's followers themselves who were the cause of so much trouble. A great many wars were fought in the name of Christ, Muhammad or some other Messenger of God. We cannot blame the Manifestations of God for this. All of Them instructed Their followers to treat everyone with love. The cause obviously lies with Their followers, who began, at some stage, to think that only their own Prophet was a Messenger of God and that only He had spoken the truth.

This idea is the cause of the tremendous prejudice which built up against anyone who did not accept that particular religion. People did not even make an effort to get to know the followers of other religions first. They had already been dubbed a bunch of heathens. Without even having a chance to explain their beliefs, they were classed as heretics whom it was a good idea to kill off from time to time.

And this is not just history. Unfortunately, there are still people who feel that only their religion contains the truth. You only have to look at Iran where, even as I write this, Ayatollah Khomeini still insists that there will never be another Messenger of God after Muhammad. To this intolerant man the Bahá'ís are therefore the enemies of God, and God does not mind if such enemies are killed.

In this way you can see that religious prejudice has often been the cause of war. According to the teachings of Bahá'u'lláh, if we wish to remove the cause, we must lay aside this prejudice. Because, as we said in Part I, it is not correct to say, for example, that Jesus Christ and no one else was a Messenger of God. If we do, we only cause disunity among people when what we need is unity.

Another of Bahá'u'lláh's teachings is that religion must be the cause of unity and love. If it is not, it is better to have no religion at all. Whenever a religion becomes the cause of hate and division, the most sensible thing is to keep away from it. That this was Bahá'u'lláh's opinion becomes clear if we look at the situation in Baghdad (see Chapter 11). He

went away into the mountains of Kurdistan because there was so much disunity at that time between the Bábís. This is why He emphasised to His followers that they should associate with the followers of all religions in friendship. Because in fact it does not matter whether a person is a Jew, a Muslim or a Christian. All are created by the one God.

Besides this division among religions, there is another form of division which is a great obstacle to the unity of mankind. I mean the division between those who believe in science and those who believe in religion. You often find that people who believe in science want nothing to do with religion. On the other hand, many people want nothing to do with science because scientists say things which do not fit in with what they believe – for example, with what the Bible says. This disunity is also caused by prejudice – in this case, the prejudice which says that religion must always be in conflict with science.

For instance, all the Manifestations of God have said that our souls live on after our bodies have died. Scientists say that you cannot prove this; therefore many people think there is no life after death. On the other hand, science has proved that the earth was not created in six days but that it took millions of years. Nonsense, say some Christians, because it says very clearly in the Bible that God created the world in six days. And since everything in the Bible is true, they say, science is wrong. So there you have a bit of a problem. Who is right and who is wrong?

Let us see what the Bahá'í Writings say on the subject. What they say is that religion and science must agree. This can come about if we continue to use our powers of reasoning. This means that the followers of the Prophets must no longer simply believe everything they are told by others. For example, it is not right to go on believing that somewhere in the universe God is sitting on a throne and that somewhere else there is a Hell where devils throw the wicked into the fire. When you think about it you realise that such things cannot exist. Bahá'u'lláh teaches that the believers should not always take writings such as the Bible too literally. I mean, do you really think that God took a rib out of Adam's body and made a woman from it? No, says 'Abdu'l-Bahá, the story of Adam and Eve must be regarded as symbolic. You should not take it literally.

On the other hand, scientists should not think that because they cannot prove something, it does not exist. This is not true either. The Bahá'í Faith teaches, therefore, that science and religion must work together. And this is quite possible because they are both concerned with knowledge. Although it is true that the scientist mainly studies those things which can be perceived by the senses, this does not matter, since religion is primarily interested in things of the spirit. This is why religion and science complement each other very nicely. One teaches us about tangible things (science) and the other about intangible ones (religion). And if both make a serious effort to respect their different fields of knowledge, unity between the scientist and the believer will come about. Then the person with faith can be a scientist and the scientist have faith.

Another great prejudice which has been the cause of much conflict is patriotic prejudice. By this is meant the opinion that one's own country is better, more beautiful, more wonderful and more important than any other. If you think about this, you will realise that this could never be the case. After all, you might have been born anywhere – perhaps on the other side of the world. Would this mean that that country was much more wonderful than the one in which you were actually born? You see how strange such an idea really is? And yet, because of such patriotic prejudice and because people have been convinced that their own country is the most important of all, many wars have been fought and millions of soldiers have died for the 'fatherland' or 'mother country'.

Rather strange, really, when you consider that God made the whole earth for all mankind. He never divided it up into countries. Man has done that himself. He hammered stakes into the ground and called that spot his own. And since people always wanted to own more land and be more powerful, they started wars. And then of course the losers did all they could to win back their pieces of land. And so it went on. Because of this, some countries have had their boundaries changed dozens of times. You only need to look at a map of Europe in 1914 to see that it was totally different from the way it is now. And on a map of Europe in 1814, a hundred years earlier, it again looked quite different.

But despite all the fuss over stakes in the ground, war has not been brought to an end. On the contrary, millions have wept over the loss of their fathers, sons or brothers who died on the battlefield. Bahá'u'lláh goes so far as to say that we should not pride ourselves on loving our country or being willing to die for it, but rather we should be proud of loving the whole world.

Of course we usually feel most at home in our own country. That is only natural because we were brought up in it and know most about it. And, in particular, we can make ourselves understood best in our own country because we normally have no language problem there. We often do not feel quite at ease in another country because we do not understand the language. Of course we can learn some foreign languages but we will never feel at home in more than a very small part of the world.

Since this is quite a serious problem, Bahá'u'lláh has said that there should be an international language. If everyone were to learn this in addition to their mother tongue, the problem would be solved. No one would have

Will he get a job?

to learn more than one language besides their own because they would be able to understand and be understood by people everywhere. Wherever you went, whether to China or Africa or anywhere at all, you would find people able to speak the international language and then you could talk to them and feel more at home.

If we return for a moment to patriotic prejudice, we find that there is another prejudice which is closely related to this. I am referring to racial prejudice or the belief that one people or one race is better and more important than all other peoples and races. Many wars have started because it was thought that another race was less intelligent or less important, with the result that it was permissible to exploit or even exterminate the 'inferior' race. You only need to think of how the black people were treated or what was done to Jews during World War II.

It is sad that there are still many people who look down on those whose skin is of a different colour from their own. Fortunately, more and more people are realising that the colour of our skin says nothing about our moral character. In every race there are good people and some who are not so good. Skin colour has nothing to do with moral character.

In fact, Bahá'u'lláh makes it clear that in God's eyes all are equal, no matter what their race, and that God makes no distinction between races or peoples. The only thing which matters to Him is whether a person loves his fellow men and wants to serve them. It is only such people that the world needs. It is totally unimportant whether the person is German, Chinese or Brazilian. All are children of

God and the different skin colours of humanity simply make the world a more attractive place. It would be rather boring if everyone were the same, just as a garden with nothing but red tulips in it would be uninteresting. So let us get rid of this prejudice, too, because until we do we shall not be able to achieve unity.

There is yet another prejudice which is a major cause of war and conflict. This is political prejudice, or the notion that one particular political system is the best. Many politicians think that their own political system is the ideal one. Whether they are communists, socialists, capitalists or liberals, they all think their own system is the best. Such an attitude inevitably leads to conflict. As long as this lasts, war will not cease and unity will be a long way off.

By now it will probably be obvious that Bahá'u'lláh abhors the use of violence. This does not mean that I should just sit back and watch if you are attacked. No, it is my duty to protect you from your attacker. Equally, Bahá'u'lláh says that if a country is attacked, it is the duty of all the other nations of the world to come to its defence. For example, if France were to invade Spain, all other countries should unite to support it against such an attack. If this were done, no country would dream of going to war. It would know in advance that it would have to reckon with the opposition of the whole world and so could never win.

Bahá'u'lláh, therefore, stressed the necessity of forming an international organisation at the earliest possible opportunity to unite the nations. Only then could peace be maintained. We now have an organisation which in some ways resembles the one envisaged by Bahá'u'lláh, i.e. the

United Nations, but it has not yet succeeded in establishing peace on earth. This is because its members do not yet understand that prejudices are the major causes of conflict. Since so many of the world's leaders themselves have these prejudices, world peace has not yet been achieved. As early as 1918 'Abdu'l-Bahá said that people must first change their ideas and set their prejudices aside. So long as there are so many people who look down on other nations, races, religions or political opinions, world peace and world unity are impossible.

Bahá'u'lláh also stressed the importance of setting up an international court of justice. Then if, for example, two countries disagree they should submit their problem to the judges of this court. They will decide which country is in the right and what is to be done. This system already exists but does not always work because the country which is in the wrong pays no attention to the court's ruling and just pursues its own course of action. Therefore, Bahá'u'lláh says it is the duty of all other countries to see that the rebellious one obeys the court, if necessary by using force.

Before we leave this subject, a word on disarmament. As you know, the arms race is one of the greatest problems of today. 'Abdu'l-Bahá saw this problem coming even before World War I and He had this to say: '. . . All the governments of the world must disarm simultaneously. It will not do if one lays down its arms and the others refuse to do so. The nations of the world must concur with each other concerning this supremely important subject, so that they may abandon together the deadly weapons of human slaughter. As long as one nation increases her military . . .

budget, other nations will be forced into this crazed competition . . .' (Quoted in *Bahá'u'lláh and the New Era*, p. 157, by J. E. Esslemont).

So far we have learned that war is mainly caused by four forms of prejudice, i.e. religious, national, racial and political. In addition there are other forms of prejudice which, although they have not actually led to war, are clearly obstacles to the unity of mankind. We have already examined one of these, namely the continuing differences between science and religion. Another serious prejudice which stands in the way of unity is the notion that women are inferior to men. In the Western world people are slowly realising that this is not true but there are many countries in which women still suffer from discrimination. They are even regarded as less intelligent beings who cannot achieve nearly as much as men. What is often forgotten is that women have always had much less opportunity to develop. The Bahá'í Faith teaches that it is essential, therefore, for women to be accorded equal rights with men. They should have the same education and the same opportunities. Women are not the *same* as men: they are strong in different areas and they give their attention to important matters traditionally undervalued by society. For instance, today it is usually the women who bring up the children, look after the health of their families, and in many developing countries are responsible for growing the food. If women are enabled to develop their abilities to the full, the progress of the world as a whole will be much faster.

There is one more problem which must be solved before mankind can reach a state of well-being and unity.

No time for play: child construction workers in Colombia

Bahá'u'lláh points to the great contrast between the rich and the poor. This difference is one of the greatest causes of discontent, envy and even of hatred. So we should not be surprised if those who are almost dying of hunger become rebellious and angry when they see how others indulge themselves with everything they want. It is absolutely unjust that such circumstances should exist all over the world in this day and age.

Let us consider the rich countries which spend millions on all kinds of weapons of destruction but are too mean to give enough money or aid to poorer countries. And then there are the rich countries which send a certain amount of financial aid but many of which regard this as loans to be repaid in a few years. Can this be called justice? All of us wonder at times how it is possible for thousands of kilos of food to be dumped by one country while thousands of people are starving to death in another. We all know this happens. But how does it happen? In our own Western countries everything is well organised but when it comes to poorer countries, suddenly we are unable to organise things. It is all too difficult and complicated.

The cause of this is clearly our lack of love for the people of other countries. This is why Bahá'u'lláh teaches us to love the whole world and not just our own country. Because no people is more important than any other people. If we think that, then we are back to national prejudice, which, as we have seen, has already caused quite enough war and bloodshed.

Apart from this, there is also the tremendous contrast between the rich and poor of one country. This situation is equally wrong and must certainly be changed. And here it is important not only to combat poverty but also to do something about excessive wealth. This can be achieved through making laws to ensure that extremes of both poverty and wealth are eliminated. It is over seventy years since 'Abdu'l-Bahá proposed that the rich should pay more tax than those who did not have so much. This proposal has already become reality in Western countries but there are still large areas of the world where it is not practised. In those countries it makes no difference whether you are a millionaire or on the bread-line; everyone pays the same percentage of tax. I do not have to explain to you that such a practice is unjust.

The last paragraph, in particular, makes it clear that Bahá'u'lláh places great emphasis on justice. As long as there is injustice, people will continue to be oppressed and ill-treated. A sense of justice is therefore very important. If we have it we shall no longer be occupied in furthering our own ends, but our first concern will be for the well-being of all mankind. We shall no longer be indifferent to the poor and the sick. We shall stand up for those who are persecuted because of their religion or imprisoned and tortured for their opinions. We shall aid the hungry and the oppressed. We shall work together to get rid of injustices and to promote human well-being instead.

When we talked of equality between men and women we saw how important it was to give girls a good education. Naturally this also applies to boys. Only when every child has a good education will the world really change. As long as children are taught to be proud of being Italian or

American or British or Japanese there will not be much progress. Unfortunately, there are still many countries in which children are told that their race or religion or land is the best in the world. Bahá'u'lláh explains that the aim of education should be quite different. Children should be brought up in the belief that 'the earth is but one country, and mankind its citizens'. His aim is to produce people who will devote their energies to the betterment of the world. These are the only kind of people the world needs.

Therefore, children should not only be filled up with facts about science, grammar, geography and so on. After all, what use is a person who knows all about science but hates Jews? What use is a professor of chemistry who is prejudiced against black people? They will never improve the world. Rather, let us make sure that children have no prejudices against people of another country, race or religion. Teach them that every individual is important and capable of doing good. Teach them to love mankind, since only such children will want to work for the unity of mankind and the well-being of all peoples.

In Part I we discovered that the world's problems are so terribly complicated that no ordinary person could ever find the right answer to them all. We constantly see those who think they have found the solution squabbling with each other. The other people's solution is always useless and unworkable while their own is the best. To avoid such situations, everyone will have to realise that only God knows the purpose of His creation and only He knows how we can achieve that purpose. We must also realise that He informs us of this purpose through His Manifestations. People must also become convinced that the goal of the present age is the unity of mankind, a goal imparted to us by Bahá'u'lláh. Then, and only then, will such unity be possible. Only when we allow ourselves to be guided by what He says, will world peace be within our reach. Only when all the world's peoples work together towards this goal of world unity, will the well-being of all mankind be possible. As long as we set aside the words of our Creator and go on thinking that we ourselves know best, the problems will only increase. It is therefore absolutely necessary for people to recognise that Bahá'u'lláh is the Messenger of God for our time and that only He can provide the solution to the problems we face. Which is why Bahá'u'lláh, writing to the peoples of the world, tells us to acknowledge Him and to accept His teachings.

The teachings which God has sent us through His Messenger Bahá'u'lláh are therefore indispensable. A healthy world is only possible if we follow His teachings. If we do not, the greatest disunity will continue. And this disunity, as we have seen, is the cause of war, chaos and destruction. If we wish to stop this we must first get rid of disunity in the world. And that is only possible if every country and each individual set aside their prejudices and begin to work for the unity of mankind. Then, no more time need be spent on designing weapons of destruction. How much money is spent on these? How many billion dollars are paid for warships, fighter planes, munitions, atomic bombs and other such weapons? If we devote our energies to unifying the world, these things will no longer be needed. Then we can spend all that money on things which really make us happier and so increase the well-being of all mankind.

On average it costs about the same:

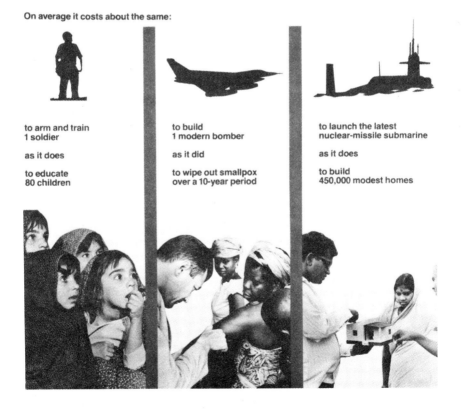

to arm and train
1 soldier

as it does

to educate
80 children

to build
1 modern bomber

as it did

to wipe out smallpox
over a 10-year period

to launch the latest
nuclear-missile submarine

as it does

to build
450,000 modest homes

These are just some of the teachings I wanted to explain which deal with the well-being of mankind. Do not think that these are all the teachings, because they are not. I have only taken the most important and even those I have gone into very briefly. This chapter should be regarded as a very short summary of all that Bahá'u'lláh and 'Abdu'l-Bahá have written on the subject. When you realise that Bahá'u'lláh alone revealed one hundred books, you will see it is impossible for me to explain it all to you in a few pages. I have had to make a small selection from the enormous number of writings which the Báb, Bahá'u'lláh, 'Abdu'l-Bahá and also Shoghi Effendi have left us.

To end this chapter, I want to look at the possibility that one day everyone will come to believe in the teachings of Bahá'u'lláh. Because I can hear you saying, when you hear about all this: 'Sounds great, but it'll never work. You'll never manage anything like that.' To which I would reply: first take a look at the history of the other religions. Look at the time of Muhammad when such fierce hatred existed between the tribes of Arabia. They were bitter enemies. And see how these tribes, under the influence of Muhammad's words, finally agreed to be friends and have now lived peaceably for centuries. Look at the time of Jesus, when there was so much division among the people and how they despised each other. And then see how these different groups became friendly with each other and lived side by side in peace for centuries. This shows quite clearly how great was the power and influence of each Manifestation of God.

And now that there is disunity once more, another Manifestation of God has appeared. Should He have less power and influence than the previous Manifestations have had? Should He not be able to create such unity? It would not make sense were Bahá'u'lláh to be the only Prophet unable to do this. If every other Messenger of God has succeeded in bringing happiness and unity to the people for whom He appeared, it is certain that Bahá'u'lláh will also succeed in establishing unity among all the peoples of the world. Because now that we are able to travel to all parts of the world and get to know each country, world unity has become possible in our time. It was different in the days of Jesus and Muhammad. Many countries had not yet been discovered and travelling long distances was difficult when you had to use a horse or even go on foot. And so world unity was an impossibility at that time. Now, however, it can be achieved. That is why Bahá'u'lláh has come to establish it. And He will obviously succeed since He is, after all, a Manifestation of God.

But perhaps you still have the question: 'All right, but how? How can it be done?' Well, there are two ways. One is the visible way and the other is invisible. Let us begin with the visible means. These are the believers themselves and their actions. They are trying to make the Bahá'í teachings known. Some of them translate or write books, give lectures or lessons in schools, make radio or television programmes, work with the United Nations, are active in child education, serve on committees or assemblies, and so on. Bahá'ís try to convey the Message of Bahá'u'lláh to everyone they come into contact with, and, above all, they try to live in accordance with the teachings of Bahá'u'lláh, which attract people to the Faith. And so, as we will see in Chapter 13, people are becoming Bahá'ís every day. The more people who become Bahá'ís, the more there will be to work for the unity of mankind. And the number of people who can tell others about the teachings of Bahá'u'lláh increases all the time. And the greater it becomes, the faster the number of followers grows. And the more followers there are, the sooner will world unity be attained. This obviously stands to reason.

Besides these visible means there is another way which we cannot perceive with our senses. That is the power of the Manifestation of God Himself which begins to exert a growing influence on people. This is the power through which all the Manifestations of God were able to influence people's thinking and change it. At first, this influence is not so strong. But gradually it becomes stronger and stronger. Just like the power of the sun: at the beginning of the day it is relatively weak but as the day advances it becomes stronger. The spiritual power of the Manifestations is like this. Gradually, each year this increases and so exerts a greater influence on people's thinking year by year. Eventually this power will become so great that everyone will turn to it.

A lot of people do not believe in this spiritual power of the Manifestations of God because they cannot see it. But in Chapter 1 we came to the conclusion that even things we cannot perceive with our senses can exist. I cannot see your thoughts but they exist nonetheless. I cannot see anger either. I cannot say I have a bagful of anger in the boot of my car. Nor can I go into a shop and ask for a pound of honesty. Yet I know that anger and honesty exist. I can see that from people's behaviour. I can see someone getting red in the face or hear it when he starts shouting. I can also see that you are a person who divides up his sweets fairly.

Power is something like this. You cannot see it but it exists. For instance, you cannot see electric power. The only thing you see is a lamp burning, in other words, the *effect* of electric power. You cannot see the earth's power of attraction either. But you can see the effects of gravity. The spiritual power of the Manifestation of God is just like this. Although we cannot see this power itself, we can see its effects.

We can see that the teachings of Bahá'u'lláh are gradually becoming reality in this world. We can see by people's behaviour that they have been influenced by this power. We can hear from what they say that people are beginning to think differently. We can see they are beginning to put aside their prejudices and stop looking down on those belonging to a different religion, nationality or race. We can see the different religions coming closer together and the countries of Europe getting along better with each other. We can see that there are organisations like the European Economic Community (EEC), the United Nations Organisation, the Organisation of African Unity (OAU), the Council for Mutual Economic Aid (COMECON), the Save the Children Fund, the World Wildlife Fund and many others. We see in more and more countries that women are obtaining the same rights and opportunities as men. In some countries the worst extremes of poverty are disappearing and they have indeed enacted laws to remove it. There are organisations like Amnesty International that try to help political prisoners and anyone else who is oppressed. We see peace movements and other groups whose aim is disarmament. Slavery and child labour have almost disappeared, and many more people are concerned to give their children a good education. We see a great number of things which are new – so many things which we should never have seen had we lived a hundred and fifty years ago.

I can see the effects of Bahá'u'lláh's spiritual power so clearly that I cannot understand how so many people can be so pessimistic about the future. The Bahá'ís are much more optimistic about it. They are aware that this spiritual power is growing year by year and therefore that unity will certainly be achieved. Besides, 'Abdu'l-Bahá Himself has assured us that 'in this marvellous cycle the earth will be transformed . . . Disputes, quarrels and murders,' He writes, 'will be replaced by peace, truth and concord; among the nations, peoples, races and countries, love and amity will appear. Cooperation and union will be established, and finally war will be entirely suppressed . . . Strong and weak, rich and poor, antagonistic sects and hostile nations . . . will act toward each other with the most complete love, friendship, justice and equity' (*Some Answered Questions*, chapter 12, pp. 63–4). Do you need any clearer proof than this? Bahá'ís do not.

*We
are
the
world*

8

Teachings for the happiness of mankind

Before dealing with these teachings there is something I should like to explain. It will not surprise you to hear that most of the teachings relating to the well-being of mankind are also intended for the individual. So if I say the world should put aside its prejudices, of course I also mean that each individual should set aside his or her prejudices. The teachings mentioned in Chapter 7 are therefore not only for the world to follow, because 'the world' does not exist. We, the people, are the world. So we shall have to find out which teachings we can follow. Which teachings, for example, can we follow individually? That is what is important.

Bahá'u'lláh does not really expect us to sit down and draw up a set of laws to combat poverty. We can do so, of course, but there will not be much point. What does make sense, however, is giving up our own prejudices. For one person this will mean doing his best to get rid of feelings of contempt for another country or people. For another it may mean he will no longer look down on women. And for yet another it may mean he begins to believe in the existence of

God. It is different for everyone. What I am concerned about is that you will not think: 'What wonderful teachings! I'm glad they're meant for the world and not for me.' Because this is not so. I'm sorry, but the old saying still holds good: if you want to improve the world, begin with yourself.

In the previous chapter we saw that Bahá'u'lláh gave humanity a goal. That goal, He tells us, is the unity of mankind. We should therefore see its attainment as the Will of God for this age. In order to attain this goal, God has given us teachings through His Manifestation. If we follow these, the unity of mankind will become a reality. However, through His Manifestation God has also given us another goal. This goal is for each individual. It is the purpose of our life. And to attain this goal we have also been given teachings. These are the teachings we shall deal with in this chapter.

Before going into these, however, let us consider this personal goal for a moment. The first thing we need to know is that a person's life consists of three parts. The first is the period before birth or the life in the womb. The second is the period between birth and death, or life on earth. And the third is the period after death, or life in the next world.

Now, the child in the womb knows nothing of life in this world. It cannot visualise the world into which it will be born. It probably is not aware that such a world exists. The same applies to people here on earth. We know nothing about the next world. Nor can we visualise life after death. We only know that that life exists because the Manifestations

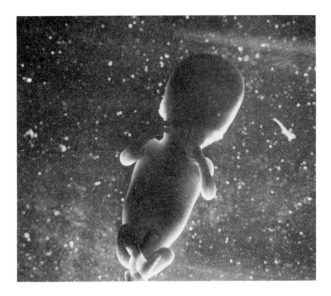

of God have told us so. They have told us of the existence of this invisible world.

However, it is also true that it is most important for the child in the womb to develop certain qualities while it is there. When it is born it is going to need these qualities. For example, a baby must be able to see, hear and feel and the brain must be properly developed. These things must be acquired in the womb. Fortunately it is not up to the baby itself to decide whether or not to develop these mental and physical capacities. It happens of its own accord whether the baby likes it or not. And a good thing too, since if the child lacks one of these capacities, life in this world will be a lot more difficult for him or her. Clearly a child who is born blind will have much more trouble than a baby that can see. It is therefore essential that every child should develop these capacities properly. If not, the child will not be able to do all the things he wants to do. Such capacities are necessary for us to function properly here on earth.

In practically the same way, this is how things work for the next world too. If we want to function properly there and feel at home, we shall have to develop certain qualities. And these qualities must be acquired here on earth. If not, the same applies as for a child who is born deaf, for example – things will be much more difficult for us in the next world. But this time it is possible for each human being to decide whether or not to develop such qualities. This is left to the individual. It does not happen of its own accord.

So there are many people who have no desire at all to develop themselves – it is too much trouble. However, if you talk to people who have taken the trouble to develop these qualities, the story is quite different. Such people are always happy that they have made the effort. Just as happy as the baby who has the ability to see, even though he made no effort to develop it. But just imagine that he had not wanted to develop this capacity. How sorry he would be when he was born.

In order that we shall have no regrets when we reach the next world, God has always made it clear through His Manifestations how important it is for us to develop those qualities of the spirit. That is the purpose of our life. That is the personal goal of every human being – to develop qualities which we need essentially for life in the next world. And since the next world is the world of God, Bahá'u'lláh calls such qualities divine. In addition, these divine qualities are needed in this world. And they are certainly meant for this too. The purpose of life is still to develop divine qualities. We shall now discuss what these are and how you can acquire them.

It does not matter which qualities you want to develop, just as long as you have the will to do it. If you want to play the piano well or learn how to draw, you must be enthusiastic about it. The best performers, artists and craftsmen are those who love their work. You know, for instance, that if you want to learn dancing the first thing you need is to be fond of dancing. The next important thing is to find a good dancing school and a good teacher. You must like going to dancing school and it is particularly important to get on well with the teacher. If you do not, it makes everything more difficult.

Well, all this also applies to the development of our divine qualities. In the first place we must want to do it and then we must find a good school and a good teacher. The Bahá'í Faith is such a school and Bahá'u'lláh is such a teacher. We must get along well with Him or we will not get very far. Just as a music teacher is necessary for us to develop our piano playing, likewise a divine teacher is indispensable for the development of our divine qualities. And Bahá'u'lláh also wants His pupils to be enthusiastic, hard-working and dedicated. Only then will we obtain the best results. Not otherwise.

For this reason it is very important for every individual to choose Bahá'u'lláh for himself. If we choose Him just because our parents have chosen Him, we are merely copying them. If we do not choose Him because our friends have not done so either, then we are letting our friends make up our minds for us. And that is not how it is meant to be. The important thing is that we should make our own decision independently of anyone else. We do not take art lessons just because our parents want us to. Nor do we give up athletics just because our friends are not keen on it. What matters is whether we ourselves want to do it. This is the reason why Bahá'u'lláh says that we must investigate the Bahá'í Faith independently. And that we must recognise Him with our own eyes as a Manifestation of God. Because He only wants pupils who are motivated, pupils who choose Bahá'u'lláh for themselves as their divine Teacher, pupils who, with His help, want to discover what divine qualities they possess. And, of course, pupils who want to learn from Him how they can develop these qualities. Dedication is therefore necessary to our development.

As you know, every Manifestation of God has had an enormous influence on human thought. This influence is stronger, however, when we accept Him as our divine Teacher. From that moment onwards, He ensures that we receive more spiritual strength than we did before. This is good, because without this strength from Him it is much more difficult for us to develop our divine qualities. So Bahá'u'lláh does not leave us to do it all by ourselves. No, He promises to help us and to give us the strength we need for our spiritual development.

This spiritual power is a sign of His love for us. In order to receive this love from Him, we must first come to love Him. When we begin to feel love for Bahá'u'lláh we will find that it becomes easier to love other people too. We now have the strength for this. Spiritual power from Bahá'u'lláh. This love for other people is actually one of the divine qualities which we need to develop. I say 'develop' because it is not so easy to love everyone just like that. It takes more than one or two days to achieve. But this is the case with everything else we have to learn. It is also impossible to become a champion swimmer in one day. It takes quite a few years. But it does not matter. As long as we can see we are making progress, it is all right. We can be happy each time we make some improvement. And we will improve because, after all, we are being helped by the Manifestation of God Himself, Bahá'u'lláh.

Choosing Bahá'u'lláh, therefore, also means choosing to develop our spiritual qualities. That will become the main purpose of our lives. So we must avoid anything which would prevent us from achieving our goal. For example, we will need to shake off thoughts like: 'Look after Number One and never mind the rest.' If we do not, we will not be able to develop spiritual qualities like loving other people. As long as we think we are the most important person and are bent on making life as pleasant as possible for ourselves, we will not have much time for others. If we only want to make ourselves happy, we cannot make others happy. It is impossible. If all we want is to have as many things as we can ourselves, we can give nothing to others.

What we have to put aside, therefore, are ambitions for wealth, possessions and power. These must be replaced by the desire to give and to make others happy. Bahá'u'lláh assures us that only then will we be really happy. How many people are there who have lots of money but are absolutely miserable? One man is constantly quarrelling with his wife because she complains that he is neglecting her, another keeps losing his friends because all he can talk about is himself; yet another is abandoned by his own children because he never took a real interest in them. All these are sad situations which could be changed, however, if people took the trouble to develop spiritual qualities.

I am well aware that this is no easy thing to do. But if we are honest, we must confess that we all like to know that someone is thinking of us, cares about us and loves us. We all love to receive love. As much as we can get. However, it is impossible to receive love if we do not wish to give it ourselves, or think about others. So if we do want love, we shall have to develop two spiritual qualities first. The first is the ability to love. The second is the ability to rid

ourselves of selfish desires. The ability to set aside the thought that 'I am the most important person and the rest must take care of themselves'.

If we want to play the guitar well and have found a good teacher, we will do exactly what he tells us. After all, he knows best which is the quickest way for us to learn properly. So we accept his authority and we do what he asks. In spite of this, however, there will be times when we do not really understand why we have to do all those boring exercises. But we do them because we know they must be of some use. Otherwise the teacher would not ask us to do them.

It is the same with Bahá'u'lláh, the divine Teacher. When we become His pupils we are working on the principle that He knows best what spiritual qualities are and how we can best acquire them. So we accept His authority and we do what He asks. And yet we may come across teachings whose purpose we do not understand. However, since we know that Bahá'u'lláh did not come to tease us, but to make the world a happier place for us and others, we obey Him anyway.

This does not mean that we should accept everything without question or do things without thinking first. No, Bahá'u'lláh expects us to do our best to find out why He asks us to do things. Just like our guitar teacher. If we do not understand why we have to do an exercise, we should ask him to explain it to us. When he does, we may still not understand it fully. But this does not mean that we must not practise it. This would be stupid and our teacher would probably ask us to take lessons from someone else. Because he knows that if we do not learn the exercises, he cannot make a good guitar player out of us.

Exactly the same applies to the Manifestation of God. The first thing He expects of us is obedience. But He also wants us to discover why He has given us a particular teaching to follow. What is the wisdom of it? We should keep asking ourselves this question. Because when we find out, we will then notice that it is much easier to follow. Because then we will understand that the teaching is good for us.

Another spiritual quality is the ability to serve one's fellow men. This capacity cannot be developed overnight either. As far as that goes, the same applies as for the capacity to love others. We can only develop our capacity for service step by step. So no one expects you to pack your bags and set out for Africa tomorrow morning to help those in need. No, one can serve others in quite small ways. Perhaps you can visit a sick neighbour or a lonely uncle. Or something like that; it does not matter what. The main thing is that you do it to be of service to that person, to help him. Because if you were to do it, for example, for the money you might receive, this is not being of service. You are only doing it for yourself.

Bahá'u'lláh says it does not matter what we do as long as we do it to serve mankind. Even if we only deliver the newspapers, it does not matter. If we do it to serve other people, that is splendid. The person who wants to become a doctor with the idea of earning as much money as possible is not serving mankind in the eyes of God. On the other hand, the person who becomes a doctor in order to serve his fellow men is indeed developing this spiritual quality. It is true that both doctors do the same work but their reasons for doing it are quite different. And it is the reason which is important. That is what matters to Bahá'u'lláh. Not whether what we are doing is important but whether we are doing it to be of service to someone. That is what counts.

The capacity to love other people goes with quite a number of other spiritual qualities. There is the capacity to be friendly, hospitable and courteous. Or the capacity to be pleasant in dealing with people. And what about the ability to encourage others? These are all fine qualities when we find them in another person. But we can also develop them ourselves.

How do you think other people have acquired them? It did not happen of its own accord although some people seem to have been born with unselfish qualities. Of course their education, too, has played an important part, but even as children such people must have been making efforts to be nice to people.

However that may be, every individual has such spiritual capacities. Including you. And for this reason alone you are special. All right, these qualities are not so well developed in some people as they are in others. And we will find that no one has developed all these qualities to an equal extent. A person could be very hospitable but not so kind to his children. Another might be very good to his children but not very hospitable. As long as we do not say: 'Well, that's too bad for the children or the visitors!' Because that is what people often say. 'That's the way I'm made and there's nothing I can do about it.' Because that is not true.

Everyone can develop these qualities. If only they want to. But you knew that already.

Another spiritual quality we should try to develop is to look for the good qualities in others and to refrain from criticising their bad qualities. It is certainly not easy to put into practice because we have become used to noticing other people's failings and talking about them. Generally, we do not let that bother us until one day we hear that someone has been gossiping about us. Then we get angry. And justifiably. It becomes really boring and is very negative to talk of nothing but people's faults. It does no good at all. Perhaps it is a fine way to hide our own faults and uncertainties from the world. There may even be people who criticise others to show themselves in a better light. And it may work.

However, Bahá'u'lláh teaches that backbiting, as it is called, is one of the worst things we can possibly do. On this subject 'Abdu'l-Bahá says that we must learn always to see the good in others. If we meet someone who has ten good qualities and one bad one, we must try to see the ten and forget the one. And even if we meet someone with ten bad qualities and only one good one, we must try to see the one good quality and forget the ten bad ones.

In any case, we must try to develop the habit of never saying unkind things about others. It is not easy and I am afraid I do not always succeed myself, but we really need to try if we are to make the world a better place and other people a little happier.

It will be obvious now that those who think they are the most wonderful people cannot really make any progress in developing their spiritual qualities. Rather it is those who search for the hidden spiritual jewels within in order to polish them and make them shine, who will get results. This too, is a quality – that of being humble and not feeling one is better than anyone else. You could compare this with your guitar lessons. As soon as you think you are playing really well, you stand still. Only those who keep looking for ways to improve themselves will make progress. Of course there are always people who cannot play as well as you do but there are also plenty of people who play much better. So it is no use looking at what other people can do. Just look at yourself, at your own jewels and learn to love them. They are worthwhile. So be content with them. Look after them. Try to bring them out and make them shine for your fellow men. That is what Bahá'u'lláh demands.

The final spiritual qualities I want to discuss, Bahá'u'lláh calls trustworthiness and sincerity. The first is of the greatest importance to the security and tranquillity of the world. When you know you can trust another person completely you will have no more fear, and when fear goes it is replaced by a feeling of security and peace. This is obvious and needs no further explanation.

The development of the second quality, sincerity or honesty, is equally important. It is in fact so important that without it we will fail to develop other qualities. 'Abdu'l-Bahá says that not until we have acquired the quality of sincerity will we be able to acquire the other spiritual qualities. Sincerity is therefore the basis of all these qualities. When we have developed this we can develop all the others. It is therefore particularly important that we try our best to become honest and sincere people. Because only then can we develop the other qualities to the full.

If we think about the foregoing, we come to the following conclusion. God has given every human being the potential to develop the qualities of, for example, love, sincerity, humility, helpfulness, service and kindness to all mankind. These qualities are divine and therefore perfect. Bahá'u'lláh then teaches us that we must be content with these capacities and it is our duty to bring them out and develop them. This does not happen of its own accord. But everyone can do it. So everyone is capable of developing these hidden qualities. There are no exceptions. Everyone can fulfil this duty if he or she makes the effort. That is the purpose of life. To make an effort to develop our divine qualities, to grow spiritually and in this way to become good, kind and worthwhile people. Both in this world and in the next.

Have we now come to the end of all the teachings for the individual? Certainly not! If I were to include all of them here and explain each of them, it would take years. Bahá'u'lláh has also given us a large number of teachings which apply only to our life here on earth. For example, His teachings with regard to marriage, divorce, sex, health and healing, drugs, hygiene, economics, work and occupations, art, the treatment of criminals, evolution, the soul and many more subjects. Hundreds of books have already been written on these topics. Not only by Bahá'u'lláh, but also by the Báb, 'Abdu'l-Bahá and Shoghi Effendi. I can assure you that if I were to go over all these teachings, this book would be about ten metres thick! And that would be a bit much for an introduction.

SELECTIONS FROM THE WRITINGS OF ABDU'L-BAHÁ

THE SECRET OF DIVINE CIVILIZATION

BAHÁ'Í WORLD FAITH

TABLETS OF BAHÁ'U'LLÁH

SELECTIONS FROM THE WRITINGS OF THE BÁB

Some Answered Questions

FOUNDATION OF WORLD UNITY

THE KITÁB-I-ÍQÁN — The Book of Certitude

EPISTLE TO THE SON OF THE WOLF

BAHÁ'Í ADMINISTRATION · SHOGHI EFFENDI

CITADEL OF FAITH · Messages to America 1947-1957

The ADVENT of DIVINE JUSTICE

The World Order of Bahá'u'lláh

MESSAGES TO THE BAHÁ'Í WORLD · SHOGHI EFFENDI

TOKENS
From the Writings of Bahá'u'lláh

Selected and illustrated by Jay and Constance Conrader

III
THE HISTORY OF
THE BAHÁ'Í FAITH

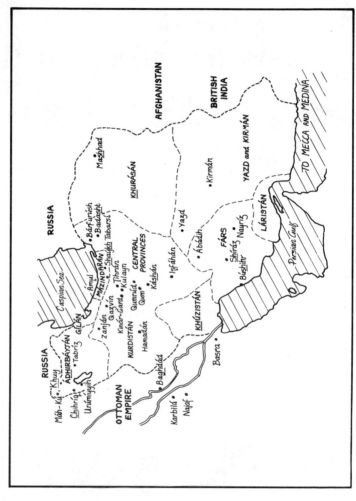

Persia in the nineteenth century

9

Background

As I said earlier, a new Manifestation of God always appeared among people whose religion had fallen into decay. What does this mean? What are the signs which tell us that a religion is in decay?

Firstly, a real feeling of love in people for God and for His Manifestations has practically disappeared. And whenever love for anyone, including the Messenger of God, disappears, people have much less inclination to do something for Him, in other words, to try to live in accordance with His teachings. Then, they only want to please themselves and leave other people to sort out their own problems.

Yet despite this lack of love for others, people often say they believe in God. But this is only in name, it seems to me. Their deeds show that these people do not really believe at all. They may go to church or mosque, temple or synagogue each week, but this is usually the only sign that they belong to any faith. Most of them are unable to put it into practice in their daily lives. In general, they are only concerned with their own wishes and desires. And if they do something for another, it is often with the thought of some profit for themselves.

This was more or less the situation in Persia when Bahá'u'lláh, the new Manifestation of God, was born there in 1817. It was easy to bribe government officials, some of whom were exceedingly cruel. The members of the clergy were mostly fanatical and intolerant. And the people were often superstitious and ignorant.

Most of the Persians were followers of Muhammad (Muslims) but there were also some followers of Zoroaster, of Moses (Jews) and of Christ. In spite of the fact that their Prophets had taught these people to live in love and harmony, they hated and despised one another. They cursed each other unashamedly, calling one another 'dirty dogs' or 'filthy heathens'. Things were so bad that it was even dangerous for a Jew or a Zoroastrian to walk in the rain. If they touched a Muslim accidentally with their wet clothes, he might be so insulted that he would kill them. The Muslims themselves were also divided into sects which were bitterly opposed to one another. Besides all this, the education of children was neglected, and pillaging and stealing were the order of the day.

Yet in spite of these dreadful conditions there were still a few people to be found who waited longingly for the coming of the promised Messenger of God. Two of these were famous teachers who were convinced that the Promised One would soon come. Their names were Shaykh Aḥmad and Siyyid Kázim. Since they were so well known for their learning, quite a number of people believed in what they said and prepared themselves for the coming of the Promised One.

It was not only in Persia but also in Europe and America

that, at the beginning of the nineteenth century, more and more people began to expect the return of Christ. For some time Christians all over the world had been dreaming, thinking and talking of the Advent or Coming of the Lord. At this time a number of Adventist movements came into existence whose members had studied the Bible deeply and become convinced that the Second Coming of Christ was about to take place. The leader of one of these movements, William Miller, even announced that it would happen between 21 March 1843 and 21 March 1844. At that time many people interpreted the Bible literally. They therefore expected to see Christ coming again on a cloud in the heavens. They also thought that many angels would appear to take the good up into Heaven, while devils would take the bad down to Hell. And if you thought that you were one of the good people, you could even buy special robes in America at that time to wear for the 'Day of Judgement', since naturally you would want to be dressed properly for the occasion.

And then came the final day: 21 March 1844. The expectant looked upwards. Some were afraid. Others prayed. Then evening came and night fell. The day was over and no sign of the Second Coming had been seen. The whole of America laughed them to scorn and the Adventists, of course, were deeply disappointed. And yet, one year later, William Miller was still insisting that the year he had announced was the correct one. According to him, Christ must have appeared in one way or another in 1844, but unseen.

But what is so remarkable is that the year 1844, the year

in which Miller claimed the greatest event in history would occur, was the year in which the Bahá'í Faith began.

You probably know that each religion has its own calendar and that the first year of that calendar is the approximate year in which the religion originated. The Christians are living in the year 1987, the Muslims in the year 1407 and the Jews in the year 5745. The Bahá'í Faith also has its own calendar. And its first day? 21 March 1844! William Miller calculated it accurately. It was only a pity that he and so many others had taken the Bible so literally in other ways. Because of this hardly any of the Christians had expected the new Manifestation of God to be born among the people just like Christ Himself had been.

Now I do not know whether you are well versed in what the Bible says, but before Jesus Christ began to teach the people another prophet lived, called John the Baptist. John told everyone the good news that the Messenger of God (Christ) would soon appear. Buddha also had a forerunner who announced His coming. And the Bahá'í Faith had its herald, too, to announce the coming of Bahá'u'lláh. His name was the Báb, and Christians who have become Bahá'ís recognise in Him the return of John the Baptist, although the Báb was not merely a herald. He was also a Manifestation of God, the Promised One of Islam, Who founded an independent religion, the Bábí religion. However, the history of the Bahá'í Faith begins with the Báb since it was His primary purpose to bring the good news that very soon after Him the Promised One of all religions, Bahá'u'lláh, would appear.

10

The Báb
1819–1850

On 20 October 1819 a son was born to a well-known merchant of the city of Shiraz, in Persia. He was called 'Alí-Muḥammad, later to become known as the Báb. His father died soon after his birth and the boy was brought up by an uncle who was also a merchant. As a child He learned to read and write and was sent with other children to a teacher of religion. During these lessons the little boy quickly attracted attention, since not only did He ask very difficult questions, but He answered them Himself. He did this so well that his teacher was dumbfounded. Later, when 'Alí-Muḥammad announced that He was the promised Manifestation of God, His uncle immediately believed in Him. Even as a child, He was extremely kind and helpful. And later, when, at the age of fifteen, He Himself was a merchant, He became known as a person of great goodness and one who lived His life in full accord with the teachings of the Prophet Muhammad. Seven years later 'Alí-Muḥammad married and had one son who, to the great sorrow of his parents, died when he was only a baby.

In 1843 Siyyid Kázim, whom we have already mentioned, died. As you know, he was a famous teacher who was convinced that the Promised One of Islam would shortly appear. Just before his death he told his disciples to go out into the world in search of the Promised One. Because the disciples did not know who the Promised One was or where He lived, they first prayed to God to help them to find Him.

One of them, called Mullá Ḥusayn, had fasted and prayed for forty days when he suddenly felt an urge to travel to the city of Shiraz. He started off at once and on 22 May 1844 arrived at the city gate of Shiraz. Now Shiraz was not a small town; on the contrary it was one of the largest cities of Persia. Where was Mullá Ḥusayn to look? It might be months before he could find the Promised One, especially as he did not even know His name. He would not recognise Him on the street, either, since he had never seen Him.

Shiraz, a nineteenth-century photograph

Suddenly, a young man came up to Mullá Ḥusayn and greeted him so warmly, it was as if they had been lifelong friends. It was also clear that this young man had awaited Mullá Ḥusayn's arrival because He at once invited him to come to His home. Surprised at this strange meeting, Mullá Ḥusayn accompanied Him. Soon afterwards he was seated with his host in a small upstairs room of His house.

There it was that 'Alí-Muḥammad, just twenty-five years old, declared to Mullá Ḥusayn that He was the Promised One and also the Herald of One much greater than Himself. From that moment onwards, He called Himself the Báb (Gate), since He was the Gate through which to enter the new age, the Bahá'í Era. The age during which the earlier Messengers of God had promised the coming of the great Universal Teacher was past. The time in which these promises would be fulfilled had begun. In 1844, just as William Miller and so many others had expected. 'This night,' said the Báb to Mullá Ḥusayn, 'this very hour, will in days to come be celebrated as one of the greatest and most significant of all festivals.'

That same evening, Mullá Ḥusayn became the Báb's first disciple. He had been deeply moved by His love and the wisdom of His words. At long last he had found the Promised One and his heart's desire was fulfilled. Within a very short time from this night, seventeen other disciples of Siyyid Kázim had recognised the Báb as a Manifestation of God. Among them was one woman, a poetess, who later received the name of Ṭáhirih (the Pure). To these first eighteen disciples the Báb gave the task of spreading the new Faith throughout the land. Filled with a tremendous love for the Báb, they went on their way. And wherever they went they told people that the Promised One had come.

The Báb Himself set out for Mecca, in Arabia, where for the first time He publicly declared Himself to be the Promised One of Islam. He then returned to Persia, where He was immediately arrested since the fanatical clergy did not wish the new Faith to spread. The Báb was summoned to appear before the Governor of Shiraz where He was rebuked and even struck in the face. Afterwards He was released but not for long because, owing to the devoted efforts of His followers, His Message was spreading like wildfire throughout the country. The number of His followers (called Bábís) quickly began to grow. Even some of the priests and merchants declared their belief in Him.

All over Persia, wherever people gathered together, they talked about the Báb. Some thought he must be a heretic or a madman. Others, who had seen Him, were deeply impressed by His love and the way in which He spoke. In several villages, men and women who claimed to believe in Him were beaten. Finally there was so much unrest that Muḥammad Sháh, who ruled Persia at that time, decided to send his learned friend, Vaḥíd, to investigate the Báb and His claims. Full of confidence and determined to dissuade the Báb from making such claims, Vaḥíd set out. But he, too, was so greatly influenced by the Báb's wisdom that, after three interviews, he decided to follow Him. The Governor was thus obliged to write to the Shah informing him that His Majesty's distinguished ambassador had become a Bábí!

Furious because of the Báb's increasing power and fame, the Governor had Him arrested. At the dead of night, the superintendent of police took the Báb prisoner. However, that same night something totally unexpected happened. A devastating epidemic of cholera broke out and within hours hundreds of people had died of it. Three of the Governor's servants died and several members of his family lay on their deathbeds. In panic the Governor fled. The police superintendent then took the Báb to his own house, but when they arrived he was told his son was dying. In despair he fell at the Báb's feet and begged Him for forgiveness and solemnly promised he would resign his job. Then, when he saw that the Báb had saved his son, he sent an urgent appeal to the Governor to allow his Prisoner's release. The Governor agreed on condition that the Báb left the city.

Saved by this miracle, the Báb left for Isfahan, where He was royally received by the Governor of that city. The people, too, were wildly excited by the Báb's visit. Such was their enthusiasm that, when the Báb left the bath house, a crowd clamoured for some of the water in which He had washed. Despite this acclaim, however, the Báb knew that He would soon be a prisoner again and that before very long He would be put to death. Because of this, He had said farewell to His wife and given her His possessions. It was to be the last time He would see her.

From that time onwards, the priests indeed began to stir up the people. Fearful that they were losing their power and influence, they made the Báb out to be a heretic and an enemy of God. At last the Shah, too, had had enough of it and wished to meet personally with the Báb. His Grand

Vizier, however, feared that the Shah would also come under the spell of the Báb's personality. He craftily informed the king, therefore, that a rebellion had just broken out which was of much more importance than the fuss about this so-called prophet. The Shah believed him and cancelled the appointment with the Báb. Immediately afterwards the Báb was taken to the distant fortress of Máh-Kú and imprisoned. That was in the summer of 1847. In this way, the Grand Vizier thought, the new religion would soon come to an end.

The Báb was placed in solitary confinement in the fortress which stood high on a remote mountain. There He spent His days, far from His family and His followers.

The Grand Vizier was wrong, though. It was not long before the people of the area and even the jailer became captivated by the modesty and wisdom of the Báb. He made such an impression on them that the jailer began to allow more and more of His followers to enter the fortress. Once again, Mullá Husayn travelled hundreds of miles on foot to see his beloved Master.

Because of these events the Báb was transferred to another fortress at Chihríq, but here the same thing happened. One after the other, priests and government officials became followers of the Báb.

The Grand Vizier was at his wits' end. His whole plan had misfired. In desperation, he ordered the religious leaders of Tabriz to interrogate the Báb and to pronounce judgement on Him. Perhaps the heresy could be rooted out once and for all in this way.

But this plan also failed. The hope that the Báb would

The fortresses of Máh-Kú (above) *and <u>Ch</u>ihríq* (right)

The Shrine of the Báb on Mt. Carmel in the Holy Land, illuminated every evening in contrast to the nights the Báb spent in Máh-Kú without even a lighted lamp

give up His claims proved vain. In the presence of the Crown Prince the Báb again declared that He was the Promised One and that it was for His coming that the priests had prayed for so long. The clergy sat there, totally confused. The Báb rose and left the room; He then allowed Himself to be taken back to Chihríq.

There He wrote many books setting out His teachings and referring to the coming of Bahá'u'lláh. In addition, He wrote numerous letters to the learned divines in every part of Persia. And although the Báb had never met them, He described in detail the wrongs each had committed.

Meanwhile, during the Báb's imprisonment, eighty-one of His followers had gathered for a conference in which they officially broke with the traditions of Islam. This increased the animosity of the clergy. From the pulpit, they now incited the people to eradicate the followers of the Báb. The Grand Vizier hesitated, uncertain what to do. When, soon afterwards, the Shah died, the Grand Vizier's influence waned. The seventeen-year-old Crown Prince ascended the throne and, since he had no experience of government, he left this in the hands of the new Grand Vizier. This man at once issued an order to punish the Bábís.

The government, clergy and people then arose as one man to destroy the followers of the Báb. In remote villages they were put to the sword one by one. In other places, such as Mázindarán, they took steps to defend themselves.

Here Mullá Husayn and Quddús, the youngest but greatest of the Báb's disciples, took charge of three hundred and thirteen Bábís. Despite the smallness of their numbers and the strength of the opposing army, they managed to hold out for almost a year, mainly because of their heroism and the cowardice of the soldiers. One day about two hundred Bábís even stormed the Prince's stronghold and penetrated as far as his private rooms. There they found that the Prince had leapt out of the window into the moat and escaped, barefoot. On another occasion a handful of nineteen Bábís charged a camp in which two regiments were garrisoned. All the troops fled and their commanding officer ignominiously rushed to the Prince to report their defeat.

Finally, after eleven months of vain efforts to force the Bábís to surrender, the Prince decided on a plan of deceit. He took the Qur'án, the Holy Book of Islam, and wrote in it that they would be free from attack if they came out of their fort. He also promised to arrange their safe return to their homes at his own expense. But when the Bábís arrived at the enemy camp, most of them were put to death by the spear or the sword, or riddled with bullets. Others were seized and sold as slaves. Quddús was dragged through the streets, where the mob killed him with knives and axes.

The same happened in two other places. The promises made to the Bábís were broken there too. Vahíd, once the honoured advisor of the Shah, was bound to a horse and dragged through the streets. His head was then cut off, filled with straw and sent to the Prince for his celebrations. The homes of the Bábís were destroyed. Women and children were led past the rows of heads which had been severed from the bodies of their fathers, brothers, sons or husbands. The cruelty was unbelievable. You can imagine that when the Báb was informed of this, He was overcome with grief. For love of God and for His sake, the Bábís had voluntarily given their lives. For five months He was inconsolable and His tears never ceased. But despite this dreadful slaughter, those Bábís who were still alive remained firmly convinced of the truth of the Báb's revelation. Day by day, their steadfastness increased. The minister realised this and came to the conclusion that the only way to get rid of this movement for good would be to put the Báb to death.

Early in the morning of 9 July 1850 the Báb was speaking with one of His followers in the barracks of Tabriz when He was rudely interrupted by the officer in charge. The Báb told him that no power on earth could silence Him until He had said all that He wished to say. The officer was astonished but told the Báb to follow him.

After the Báb's death sentence had been authorised, He was bound to the wall to face the firing squad. With him was a young disciple, Anís, who had begged to be allowed to die with the Báb. The firing squad took its place in three ranks, each two hundred and fifty strong. The soldiers fired, a row at a time, until every rifle had been discharged. But when the dense smoke cleared, the ten thousand onlookers saw to their astonishment that the Báb had disappeared. Only the ropes had been severed.

A search began at once and shortly afterwards the Báb was discovered in His cell by the same officer who had earlier interrupted Him, calmly finishing His conversation with His disciple. The Báb then informed the officer that He had finished and he could now carry out his orders. Remembering what the Báb had said earlier, the officer was so frightened that he left immediately. The captain of the firing squad also refused to have any more to do with the execution and marched his men away.

Another regiment then volunteered to put the Báb to death. Once again the soldiers took their places, and this time the Báb declared to all those present that the day would come when they would recognise Him. Soon afterwards, the bodies of the Báb and His faithful companion were riddled with bullets.

At that very moment a dreadful storm arose and a violent whirlwind was unleashed on the city. Before the year was ended a terrible earthquake occurred in which 250 members of the final firing squad met their deaths, while the remaining 500 were themselves executed three years later for mutiny. The Grand Vizier also died within two years of the Báb's execution.

But the Bábís continued to spread the teachings of their beloved Master, despite His death. The fire of their love for the Báb was still burning brightly.

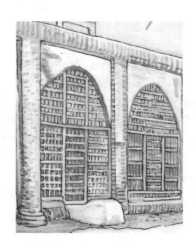

11

Bahá'u'lláh
1817–1892

On 12 November 1817 in Teheran, the capital of Persia, a son was born to a prominent minister of state, Mírzá Buzurg, and his wife Khadíjih. The boy, to whom they gave the names of Ḥusayn-'Alí, was later to be known as Bahá'u'lláh. The child led a carefree life, growing up as a member of a wealthy family who never suspected that their son might one day proclaim Himself to be the great Universal Teacher foretold by every earlier Messenger of God. Yet the father soon realised that his son was different from other children. For, although little Mírzá Ḥusayn-'Alí had never been to school and had only received some instruction at home, He was extraordinarily knowledgeable.

Before He was thirteen He was already famous at the Court for His learning. The ministers used to come to Him to discuss their problems with Him. He was already speaking at great assemblies of theologians and explaining the most complicated matters to them. But it was not only because of His knowledge that everyone came to Him. As a child He was extremely kind and helpful. Wherever people were in need, Mírzá Ḥusayn-'Alí extended a helping hand

and used to spend His time in caring for the sick and the poor. When His father died in 1839, the government wished to appoint Him as his successor but He would not accept the appointment.

Shortly before this, He had married Navváb, the daughter of another minister. Husband and wife devoted themselves to the care of the poor and became known respectively as the Father of the Poor and the Mother of Consolation. A few years later, on 23 May 1844, a son was born. They called Him 'Abbás and He later took the title of 'Abdu'l-Bahá. A short time after this event Mírzá Husayn-'Alí, who was now twenty-seven years of age, received a scroll written by the Báb. When He began to read it He realised that its Author spoke the truth and He recognised Him as the Messenger of God. Without any thought for His wealth or noble birth, He accepted the new Faith and at once began to devote Himself entirely to spreading the teachings of the Báb. Within a short time, He had already convinced many people of the truth of the Bábí message. The new believers included not only friends and members of His own family but also a number of government officials. Yet He did not escape the persecutions which were becoming increasingly cruel. Twice He was taken prisoner and on one occasion the soles of His feet were so badly lashed and beaten that they bled freely.

Then in 1852, two years after the Báb's execution, something dreadful happened. Two of the Báb's followers had been so overcome with grief at His martyrdom that, in a fit of despair, they attacked the new ruler, Násiri'd-Dín Sháh. Although the weapon they used was totally inadequate and the king was scarcely wounded, this attack triggered off the cruellest persecutions of the Bábís. At last their enemies had a 'valid' reason for taking revenge on the Bábí community with a clear conscience.

Hundreds of innocent followers were tortured and killed in the ensuing months. Many of them were even sawn in half, blown from cannon-mouths, hacked to pieces, dismembered with hatchets and clubbed or stoned. Even women and small children were put to death in the most barbaric ways. In addition, hundreds of Bábís were imprisoned. Mírzá Ḥusayn-'Alí Himself was seized and thrown into an underground dungeon known as the 'Black Pit' because it was so dark. His feet were placed in stocks and such heavy chains were hung round His neck that at the time of His passing, forty years later, the marks could still be clearly seen. He was kept in these conditions for four months. Even His food was poisoned, which affected His health for years. But this time too, the perpetrators of these terrible deeds were one by one punished by the power of God. In the years that followed, many of them died of the strangest diseases.

But let us return to the Prisoner in the 'Black Pit' for, in this cold and filthy dungeon, something very important happened to Him. 'During the days I lay in the prison of Teheran,' He wrote years afterwards, 'though the galling weight of the chains and the stench-filled air allowed Me but little sleep, still in those infrequent moments of slumber I felt as if something flowed from the crown of My head over My breast, even as a mighty torrent that precipitateth itself upon the earth from the summit of a lofty mountain.

Every limb of My body would, as a result, be set afire. At such moments My tongue recited what no man could bear to hear.' (*Epistle to the Son of the Wolf*, p. 22).

One evening He also heard a wonderfully sweet voice above Him. Looking up, He saw before Him the face of a young woman, radiant with joy. Pointing with her finger to His head, she addressed the whole of mankind, saying that this was the Best-Beloved, the Beauty of God.

Again, He had a dream in which words seemed to ring on all sides, proclaiming that He would be victorious and that there was no need to fear, for He was in safety. For Mírzá Ḥusayn-'Alí this was the summons from God to begin His Mission. It was clear to Him from this dream that He Himself was the One who would reveal God's Will and that He was the Glory of God (i.e. Bahá'u'lláh). Nevertheless, this summons had to be kept a secret for several years and He could tell no one that He was the One foretold by all the Prophets of the past.

At last, some weeks after this Revelation, Bahá'u'lláh was released from prison. The Russian ambassador to Persia had done everything he could to prove that Bahá'u'lláh could have had nothing to do with the attempt on the king's life. Besides, Bahá'u'lláh was so ill that He could scarcely stand. And, since it was unlikely He could have survived much longer, the king permitted His release. In any case, during His imprisonment, His home had been ransacked and almost destroyed.

Yet all this was insufficient punishment in the eyes of the king. He ordered Bahá'u'lláh to leave the country within a month. In spite of His ailing health, Bahá'u'lláh was forced, with His wife, two of His children – aged six and eight – and two brothers, to set out for Baghdad, which at that time was a city of the Turkish Empire. The time was January 1853 – the depths of winter. Without sufficient warm clothing, they were forced to walk hundreds of miles through mountainous regions where the ground was covered by a thick layer of snow and ice. Three months later they arrived at last, completely exhausted, in Baghdad.

As soon as Bahá'u'lláh had recovered a little, He at once began to teach those who showed any interest in the Bábí cause. He also encouraged the Bábís themselves who were dismayed by so much sadistic persecution. Soon those who had suffered so much for their faith were taking heart once more. From all directions they came to Baghdad to listen to the words of Bahá'u'lláh, Who inspired them with fresh hope and confidence in the future.

Meanwhile Mírzá Yahyá, one of Bahá'u'lláh's half-brothers, had arrived in Baghdad too. When he saw how the Bábís had come to love his Brother, he became jealous of Him. He began to spread malicious gossip about Him, causing some Bábís to turn away from Bahá'u'lláh and side with Mírzá Yaḥyá. As you can imagine, this caused Bahá'u'lláh much grief, since His aim, and that of the Báb, was to promote unity among people. Now there was disunity and discord, even among the followers of the Báb!

In order not to be the cause of disunity, Bahá'u'lláh left without warning for Kurdistan in April 1854. There He lived alone in the wilderness for two years. No one in Baghdad knew where He had gone. One day, however, His family were told by some travellers that a saintly man, whose great knowledge and wisdom were respected for miles around, was living in the mountains of Kurdistan. Even the teachers and students from a nearby seminary had so much respect for Him that some believed He must be a prophet. 'Abbás Effendi, Bahá'u'lláh's eldest son, then at once realised that such a saintly person could be none other than His own Father. He immediately wrote Him a letter, begging Him to return. Bahá'u'lláh consented and came back to Baghdad in March 1856, where He was received and embraced by His overjoyed family. He soon succeeded in inspiring the Bábís to fresh efforts and in re-establishing unity among them. The Bábí community soon became known once again for its kindness, humility, honesty, sincerity, fairness, tolerance and friendship.

During the first few months after Bahá'u'lláh's return, many friends who had come to know Him in Kurdistan also came to visit Him in Baghdad. There they joined the

Bábí community, whose reputation, because of the loving efforts of Bahá'u'lláh, now stood high. So high in fact that, from far and near, large numbers of people now came to Baghdad to see Bahá'u'lláh and hear His teachings. In His house, everyone felt happy and forgot their problems. For some, the room in which Bahá'u'lláh received his guests was like a taste of paradise. It was such a wonderful place to be. Bahá'u'lláh's love knew no bounds. He had time for all and gave His attention to everyone. No one felt left out. Gradually more and more people began to feel such a great love for Him that they became Bábís and began doing their best to live their lives according to the example set by their beloved Master.

During this period Bahá'u'lláh also wrote a number of important books which have since been translated into many languages. One of them, the *Book of Certitude*, some 200 pages long, was revealed in two days and two nights in the year 1862.

You can imagine, however, that because of all this. because of Bahá'u'lláh's increasing influence, because of the growing affection in which He was held and because of the enormous volume of writings which He revealed, the animosity and hatred of His enemies kept growing. The Persian consul-general even began to incite some of the inhabitants of Baghdad to insult Bahá'u'lláh on the street. However, whenever Bahá'u'lláh met any of them, He made a point of walking up to them, teasing them about their unworthy intentions, and leaving them covered with confusion. Angered by his failure, the consul then hired an assassin to kill Bahá'u'lláh. But when this man actually confronted Bahá'u'lláh, gun in hand, be became so frightened that he dropped the weapon. Bahá'u'lláh asked His companion to hand it back to His would-be assassin and show him the way to his home.

The priests and divines also made all kinds of plans to stamp out the Bábí religion. Once, one of their number was sent to Bahá'u'lláh to ask Him to perform a miracle as a proof of the truth of His cause. Although Bahá'u'lláh considered that they had no right to demand such a thing, He nevertheless agreed. However, they must undertake, as soon as the miracle was performed, to entertain no more doubts about Him. They must also declare in writing that He spoke the truth. The divines, however, did not wish to know the truth and abandoned their request.

Meanwhile, the consul had been in correspondence with the Shah of Persia and had convinced him that Bahá'u'lláh was preparing a revolt against him. The Persian government finally asked the Turkish authorities to remove Him as far as possible from the Persian border. Eventually, after lengthy negotiations, the Turks agreed to this. Bahá'u'lláh was invited to proceed to Istanbul, or Constantinople, as it was then called. This city was situated at the far side of the Turkish Empire, some thousand miles from Baghdad.

When the Bábís heard of this they were in despair. The majority knew they might never see Bahá'u'lláh again. The mere thought of this was so terrifying to some that they felt they would rather kill themselves. Bahá'u'lláh succeeded in calming them, however, and in addition, shortly before His departure for Istanbul, He made known the secret which He had kept for so long.

*The bridge
across the
Tigris at
Baghdad*

In the gardens of one of His friends He announced to His
followers that He was the Universal Educator promised by
the Báb and all the Prophets of former ages. He was the
Return of Christ, the Lord of Hosts, the Great Announcement, the Glory of God (Bahá'u'lláh). The twelve days He
spent in these gardens, during which He made this
announcement, are commemorated by the Bahá'ís as the
Feast of Riḍván (Paradise). On 3 May 1863 Bahá'u'lláh
left Baghdad for Constantinople.

As He departed, thousands of people lined the streets to
bid farewell to the One whose teachings and example had
had such a powerful effect on their lives for over ten years.
Some were overcome with sorrow and many wept, whether
or not they were Bábís – it made no difference. Everyone

was deeply affected. As Bahá'u'lláh rode through the streets of Baghdad, many bowed their heads before Him. Some threw themselves in front of His horse, preferring death to separation from their Beloved. Others were dumbfounded. Never before had they seen such a thing. Not even a king would receive such homage and respect.

Four months later Bahá'u'lláh and His family, accompanied by twenty-six of the believers, arrived in Constantinople. On their way they had been fêted in many towns whose citizens had gone out of their way to make the party comfortable. But in Constantinople they were allotted a small house in which there was scarcely enough room for them all. And yet here, too, many people came to visit Bahá'u'lláh to hear His teachings. And ultimately the clergy here also became afraid that the same thing as had happened in Baghdad would happen to them.

After a stay of only four months Bahá'u'lláh was informed that He was again to be banished, this time to Edirne, then known as Adrianople. Although their journey only lasted twelve days, it was nevertheless the worst they had ever experienced. The weather was so cold that even the largest rivers were frozen over, a thing which had never been known to occur. To make matters worse, the travellers had no warm clothing to protect them from the icy winds and arrived in Adrianople completely numb with the cold. Yet Bahá'u'lláh at once began to teach there, making His cause known and being accepted by most of the Bábís as the Promised Manifestation of God. From this time onwards they no longer called themselves Bábís but, instead, followers of Bahá'u'lláh, or Bahá'ís.

Meanwhile Bahá'u'lláh's jealous half-brother, Mírzá Yaḥyá, had also arrived in Adrianople. When he found how greatly loved his Brother had again become, he began plotting His downfall once more. One day, he put poison in Bahá'u'lláh's tea, making Him so ill that He suffered from intense pain and high fever for a month and a shaking hand for the rest of His life. Undeterred, Mírzá Yaḥyá then poisoned the family's well so that many of them also became ill. He even went so far as to attempt to have Bahá'u'lláh assassinated. He also informed the Bahá'ís that Bahá'u'lláh was an impostor and that he himself was the promised Messenger of God.

Bahá'u'lláh's cup was now full. With His family, He withdrew into His house in order to give each of the exiles complete freedom to choose between Him and His brother. Almost without exception they chose Bahá'u'lláh. Those who turned away from Him were a handful of Mírzá Yaḥyá's friends, but their number was so small that Yaḥyá felt totally defeated.

The Bahá'í community could breathe freely once more and now directed their energies towards the propagation of the teachings of their Master. Bahá'u'lláh Himself was fully engaged in expounding these teachings and, day and night, revealed many Tablets.

One of these was His famous letter of 1867 to the kings and religious leaders of the world, in which He called them to turn to Him and to accept His message. He exhorted them to try to settle their differences with other countries and to work for world peace. He urged them to be just, to reduce their armaments and to lower their taxes on those

who could not afford to pay. He also warned them that
terrible disasters would follow if they ignored His counsels
and remained indifferent to God's commands. Only through
His teachings could the Most Great Peace be established.
Not one of the rulers ever replied. Bahá'u'lláh's summons
was haughtily rejected by nearly all of them.

Despite all this, the number of believers kept increasing.
There were now Bahá'ís not only in Persia but also in Iraq,
Turkey, Egypt, Syria and part of Russia. This, however,
only made the opposition stronger and fresh persecutions
broke out. In Persia dozens of Bahá'ís were tortured and
killed and hundreds imprisoned. In the Turkish Empire,
too, animosity increased day by day. Alarmed at the
growing number of Bahá'u'lláh's followers and admirers,
the Sultan of Turkey banished Him, together with most of
His close followers, to the city of 'Akká, in what was then
Syria but is now part of Israel. There He was expected to
die since it was well known that hardly anyone ever left
'Akká alive.

*Bahá'u'lláh's
prison cell
in the barracks
at 'Akká*

'Akká was a prison city which housed not only the worst criminals, but was exceptionally dirty. It was infested with vermin and plagued by the most terrible diseases. In spite of Bahá'u'lláh's warning, about seventy of His family and friends went with Him of their own free will. After having spent almost five years in Adrianople, Bahá'u'lláh left on 12 August 1868 for 'Akká. Immediately on arrival, they were taken to the barracks and locked up. Soon everyone had become ill and three of the party died within a few days. Bahá'u'lláh Himself was imprisoned in a separate cell, and only His immediate family were allowed to visit Him there.

This strict imprisonment lasted for two years. During all this time it was absolutely forbidden for the Bahá'ís, even though they had walked all the way from Persia to see their Beloved, to enter the prison city. They could only catch a glimpse of Him from a distance as He stood at the window of His cell. And yet Bahá'u'lláh's sufferings were increased when one day, in the year 1870, Mírzá Mihdí, 'Abbás Effendi's younger brother, fell from the roof of the barracks and lay fatally hurt on the ground below. Bahá'u'lláh asked His son what he wished. He assured him that God could enable him to recover. But Mírzá Mihdí begged Bahá'u'lláh to accept his life as a ransom for the many Bahá'ís who were longing for the prison gates to open so that they could come in and visit Bahá'u'lláh. Bahá'u'lláh granted his wish, yet what grief it must have been to Him when his twenty-two-year-old son died a few hours later!

Soon after this tragic event, the Turkish army had need of the barracks for its soldiers and so Bahá'u'lláh and His family were transferred to a small house in the city. Here, too, Bahá'u'lláh was a prisoner and not allowed to leave the house. During these years He once again wrote numerous tablets and sent a second set of letters to the Christian rulers of Europe. Once more He called upon the Emperor Napoleon III to turn to Him, since He was the One whose coming Christ had foretold. Bahá'u'lláh also summoned him to proclaim His Revelation and to inform his people of it. He prophesied that, unless Napoleon arose in support of His Faith, his empire would be lost and he himself would be humiliated. When Napoleon received this letter, he threw it contemptuously to the ground. Less than a year later, in 1870, he was unexpectedly defeated by the Prussian army, lost his empire, was taken as a prisoner to Prussia and died in England two years later.

Czar Alexander II of Russia also received a letter in which Bahá'u'lláh warned him three times not to turn away from God and His Manifestation. Despite this warning, the Czar instituted a cruel policy of oppression which culminated in his own assassination only a few years after he had received the letter.

Pope Pius IX;
Kaiser Wilhelm I
(right)

Soon afterwards, Kaiser Wilhelm I of Germany also received a letter in which Bahá'u'lláh warned him against his haughty attitude and against withholding himelf from accepting His Revelation. In that letter Bahá'u'lláh also prophesied a time when the banks of the Rhine would run with blood and the lamentations of Berlin would be heard. As you know, some years later, the First World War broke out, in which thousands of soldiers died for the German Fatherland. And in the Second World War Berlin did indeed lament when the whole city was practically destroyed by bombs.

As a final example, let us take Bahá'u'lláh's letter to Pope Pius IX, in which He announced that He was the Manifestation of God promised by Christ. He also warned the Pope not to dispute with Him as the earlier divines had done with Jesus. He called upon him to abandon his palaces, sell his treasures and proclaim the Bahá'í message. The Pope paid no attention to this letter, however. One year later, he was forced to surrender to the Italian army which had occupied Rome. As a result, the papal kingdom was reduced to a tiny area of no more than a hundred acres.

Emperor Napoleon III (left); *Czar Alexander II*

In addition to all these letters, Bahá'u'lláh wrote the *Book of Aqdas* in 1873, in which He clearly set out His teachings. This book may be regarded as a code of laws for all mankind. In it Bahá'u'lláh describes exactly what we must and must not do if we wish to live happy and peaceful lives. If people chose to remain self-centred and unbelieving, rejecting these laws of God, Bahá'u'lláh predicted that dreadful wars and calamities would surely occur. Well, people have remained self-centred and many wars have also broken out, including the First and Second World Wars. These wars could have been prevented had people listened to the counsels given by the Manifestation of God, Bahá'u'lláh.

Meanwhile, a new governor had been appointed in 'Akká who was a good deal more humane than his predecessor. He even became very friendly towards Bahá'u'lláh. The people of the city also began to have more and more respect for the Prisoner. It was therefore not long before He was permitted visitors once more, even though the Sultan of Turkey had originally forbidden this.

In Persia, however, many Bahá'ís were still being tortured and killed. The population of Yazd were even given a holiday in order to witness how the Bahá'ís were put to death. And in the evenings celebrations were held in that city because of these deaths.

Fortunately, in 1877, Bahá'u'lláh's imprisonment in 'Akká came to an end. His son, 'Abbás Effendi, managed to rent a house outside the city. Although His Father was in fact still the Sultan's prisoner, no one objected. A few days later Bahá'u'lláh saw flowers and green trees for the first

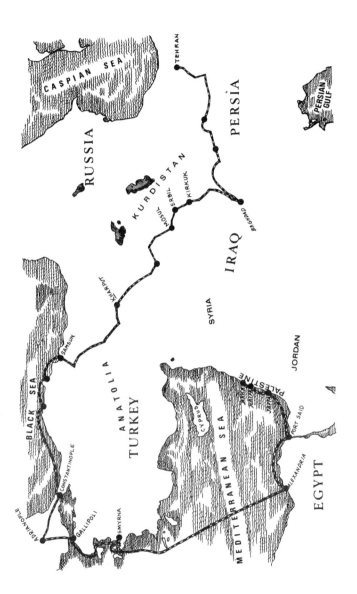

Route of Bahá'u'lláh's exile from Persia through Iraq and Turkey to the Holy Land

The Shrine of Bahá'u'lláh at Bahjí, the holiest place of pilgrimage to Bahá'ís the world over

time in nine years. Two years after this, He moved to a
nearby mansion at Bahjí. There Bahá'u'lláh lived very
simply until the end of His life. In the last twelve years
before His passing He was chiefly engaged in the writing of
many books, tablets and letters.

He rarely received visitors. His son received them on His
behalf, so that He might not be overburdened. One of the
few who were allowed to see Him was Professor E. G.
Browne of Cambridge University, who arrived in 1890.
During this visit Bahá'u'lláh spoke to him as follows: 'Thou
hast come to see a prisoner and an exile . . . We desire but
the good of the world and the happiness of the nations; yet
they deem us a stirrer-up of strife and sedition worthy of
bondage and banishment . . . That all nations should
become one in faith and all men as brothers; that the bonds
of affection and unity between the sons of men should be
strengthened; that diversity of religion should cease, and
differences of race be annulled – what harm is there in this?
. . . Yet so it shall be; these fruitless strifes, these ruinous
wars shall pass away, and the "Most Great Peace" shall
come . . . Do not you in Europe need this also? Is not this
that which Christ foretold? . . . Yet do we see your kings
and rulers lavishing their treasures more freely on means
for the destruction of the human race than on that which
would conduce to the happiness of mankind . . . These
strifes and this bloodshed and discord must cease, and all
men be as one kindred and one family . . .' (Quoted in
Bahá'u'lláh and the New Era, p. 37).

Two years later, on 29 May 1892, in His seventy-fifth
year, Bahá'u'lláh died. One of His last writings was His

Will and Testament, in which He named 'Abbás Effendi as His successor and the sole interpreter of His writings. After His passing the Bahá'ís must turn to His son and obey Him. This was the only way in which the unity of the Faith could be preserved. And that had been Bahá'u'lláh's life-long mission: to promote the unity of mankind.

12

'Abdu'l-Bahá
1844–1921

Let us go back to the night of 22 May 1844. The Báb is seated with Mullá Ḥusayn in the upstairs room of His house and, two hours and eleven minutes after sunset, announces that He is the promised Messenger of God. That same night a baby boy is born somewhere in Teheran. He is Bahá'u'lláh's son 'Abbás Effendi, later to be known as 'Abdu'l-Bahá.

As you know, His Father was thrown into an underground dungeon in 1852 and there received the Revelation of God. At that time, 'Abbás Effendi was only eight years old. Being the son of a Bábí, He was taunted by other children, who called Him the son of a heretic and threw stones at Him in the street. Once, when 'Abbás Effendi was allowed to visit His Father in captivity and saw how shamefully He had been treated, He was overcome with sorrow. From that moment onwards, He wanted to share all His Father's troubles. And these troubles began immediately after Bahá'u'lláh was released.

When the whole family was exiled to Baghdad, where the jealous Mírzá Yaḥyá caused so much trouble that Bahá'u'lláh was forced to go away into the mountains of Kurdistan, you can understand how much 'Abbás Effendi suffered as a result, especially as He did not know whether His Father would ever return. In addition, the nine-year-old boy had already realised, the very first to do so, that His Father was the promised Manifestation of God. From that time on, 'Abbás Effendi wanted nothing but to be His servant. That is why, after His Father's passing, He called himself 'Abdu'l-Bahá (the Servant of Bahá). And His servitude was such as no one can attain. As Bahá'u'lláh said, He was the perfect pupil of the Perfect Teacher, the perfect example of what a Bahá'í should be.

Soon after His Father's return to Baghdad, 'Abdu'l-Bahá became known as a boy who was both wise and loving. Day and night He was tirelessly engaged in helping others. And yet He himself was no more than a child. Later, in Constantinople and Adrianople, people began to call Him 'Master' even though He was still only twenty. Age did not matter as He received even the most learned visitors and answered the questions they had in fact wished to ask Bahá'u'lláh. However, 'Abdu'l-Bahá did not wish His Father to be overburdened and, in order to protect Him, He often took these tasks upon himself. Later on, in 'Akká, people from every walk of life, from the Governor himself to the poorest beggar, began to love and respect Him.

Immediately after their arrival in 'Akká, when everyone was ill, 'Abdu'l-Bahá looked after all the sick until He himself became so ill that for a month His life was in danger. Yet despite all the difficulties experienced in 'Akká, 'Abdu'l-Bahá also had some happy moments during this period. It was here that He married Munírih Khánum.

'Abdu'l-Bahá. A photograph taken c.1868

'Abdu'l-Bahá as Westerners saw him after his release from prison

Their union was a long and happy one. Another time of great joy was when Bahá'u'lláh was allowed to leave the prison and go to live in Bahjí.

Nevertheless, 'Abdu'l-Bahá experienced much suffering. Particularly after the passing of His Father He had a great deal of sorrow. As you know, Bahá'u'lláh had appointed Him in His Will and Testament as His successor. 'Abdu'l-Bahá was the one to whom the believers must turn and He alone was permitted to interpret His Father's writings. When 'Abdu'l-Bahá assumed this task, some of His relatives were at once offended. His half-brother, in particular, became so jealous that he began to spread all kinds of lies and even succeeded in persuading almost the whole of Bahá'u'lláh's family to take his side. 'Abdu'l-Bahá was left alone, abandoned and betrayed by His own family. His mother had passed away and His sons had also died young. Only His sister, His four daughters, His wife and an uncle remained loyal to Him. The others accused Him of exploitation and other unworthy things. Their only reason for this was that it had been He, 'Abdu'l-Bahá, and not they whom Bahá'u'lláh had appointed to succeed Him. In spite of their hatred, however, the relatives did not succeed in sowing dissension among the Bahá'ís. Nearly all Bahá'u'lláh's followers accepted 'Abdu'l-Bahá as Head of the Faith and expounder of His teachings. Many then began to carry out the assignments which 'Abdu'l-Bahá gave them.

Only one year after the passing of Bahá'u'lláh the first believers set out for the United States to teach the Faith there. The first American accepted the Bahá'í Faith in

1894, to be followed by many others. Four years later the first American believers came to 'Akká to visit 'Abdu'l-Bahá. They afterwards travelled to various parts of Europe to spread the Bahá'í teachings there, and several of them wrote down what they had seen. One man, who was not a Bahá'í but who visited 'Abdu'l-Bahá at the turn of the century, wrote a book describing 'Abdu'l-Bahá – the Master, as He was known:

> We open the window and look down. We see a crowd of human beings with patched and tattered garments. Let us descend to the street and see who these are.
>
> . . . Many of these men are blind; many more are pale, emaciated, or aged . . . Most of the women are closely veiled, but enough are uncovered to cause us well to believe that, if the veils were lifted, more pain and misery would be seen. Some of them carry babes with pinched and sallow faces. There are perhaps a hundred in this gathering, and besides, many children . . .
>
> These people are ranged against the walls or seated on the ground, apparently in an attitude of expectation: – for what do they wait? Let us wait with them.
>
> We have not to wait long. A door opens and a man comes out. He is of middle stature, strongly built. He wears flowing light-coloured robes. On his head is a light buff fez with a white cloth wound about it. He is perhaps sixty years of age. His long grey hair rests on his shoulders. His forehead is broad, full, and high, his nose slightly aquiline, his moustaches and beard, the latter full though not heavy, nearly white. His eyes are grey and blue, large, and both soft and penetrating. His bearing is simple, but there is grace, dignity, and even majesty about his movements. He passes through the crowd, and as he goes utters words of

salutation . . .

He stations himself at a narrow angle of the street and motions to the people to come towards him . . . In each open palm he places some small coins. He knows them all. He caresses them with his hands on the face, on the shoulders, on the head. Some he stops and questions . . . To all he says, '*Marhabbah, marhabbah*' – 'Well done, well done!' . . .

This scene you may see almost any day of the year in the streets of Akka. There are other scenes like it, which come only at the beginning of the winter season. In the cold weather which is approaching, the poor will suffer, for, as in all cities, they are thinly clad. Some day at this season, if you are advised of the place and time, you may see the poor of Akka gathered at one of the shops where clothes are sold, receiving cloaks from the Master. Upon many, especially the most infirm or cripples, he himself places the garment, adjusts it with his own hands, and strokes it approvingly, as if to say, 'There! Now you will do well.' There are five or six hundred poor in Akka, to all of whom he gives a warm garment each year.

On feast days he visits the poor at their homes. He chats with them, inquires into their health and comfort, mentions by name those who are absent, and leaves gifts for all.

Nor is it the beggars only that he remembers. Those respectable poor who cannot beg, but must suffer in silence – those whose daily labour will not support their families – to these he sends bread secretly . . .

All the people know him and love him – the rich and the poor, the young and the old – even the babe leaping in its mother's arms . . . He is the kind father of all the people . . .

For more than thirty-four years this man has been a prisoner at Akka. But his jailers have become his friends . . . And how could it be otherwise? For to this man it is the law, as it was to Jesus of Nazareth, to do good to those who injure him. (*The Life and Teachings of Abbas Effendi*, by M.H. Phelps, published in 1903.)

But because of all these successes, the jealousy and hatred of 'Abdu'l-Bahá's half-brother, 'Alí-Muḥammad, became intense. He himself had not managed to cause any schism in the Bahá'í community and was obliged to look on while everyone came for help and guidance to 'Abdu'l-Bahá, who was now writing numerous letters to the Bahá'ís all over the world, encouraging and advising them. And so when 'Abdu'l-Bahá was engaged in building the shrine for the mortal remains of the Báb, 'Alí-Muḥammad at once wrote a letter to the Turkish authorities. He informed them that 'Abdu'l-Bahá was constructing a fortress and that He secretly possessed an army of 30,000 with which He was about to overthrow Syria. In addition, he made a number

The Shrine of the Báb in 'Abdu'l-Bahá's time. 'Every stone of that building . . . I have with infinite tears, and at tremendous cost, raised and placed in position.'

of other dreadful accusations against 'Abdu'l-Bahá in the hope that the authorities might issue an order for His execution. No such order was issued, however. 'Abdu'l-Bahá was more strictly confined as a result, though, and no longer allowed to leave the prison city. He was constantly watched and visitors were no longer welcome.

In the face of these fresh difficulties 'Abdu'l-Bahá remained calm and continued writing letters to the believers. At times He wrote as many as ninety letters in a day, answering their questions, directing their activities and encouraging them to continue their work. He also carried on, unperturbed, the task of building the Shrine of the Báb on Mount Carmel. As a result, His half-brother's hatred grew and he continued, more fanatically than ever, to spread base lies and make outrageous accusations. Finally, he succeeded in making the authorities so nervous that in 1904 the Sultan appointed a commission to investigate the matter. 'Abdu'l-Bahá was obliged to appear in court on several occasions to hear the charges against Him. Each time He explained to the members of the commission how ridiculous such charges were, saying that the court might do with Him as they pleased. If they wished to execute Him, He would accept their decision. It would be a great honour for Him to be allowed to die for His Faith.

Three years later, in 1907, another commission was appointed. Because the four officials who formed this commission had been bribed by His enemies, 'Abdu'l-Bahá refused to meet them. After they had carried on their so-called investigation for a month, they came to a decision.

'Abdu'l-Bahá must be removed from 'Akká. At the same time, however, they heard that there had been an attempt on the Sultan's life and left at once for Constantinople, without 'Abdu'l-Bahá. When they tried to report to the Sultan that 'Abdu'l-Bahá had been found guilty and should be executed, the Sultan was no longer interested. An attempt had been made on his life and he now had more important things on his mind.

Several months later a tremendous revolution convulsed the Turkish Empire. The Young Turks gained a rapid victory and immediately announced an amnesty for all political and religious prisoners. Thus in September 1908, 'Abdu'l-Bahá's forty-year imprisonment came to an end. At last He was free to come and go as He wished. He had entered the prison city as a young man of twenty-four; now He was leaving it, an old man of sixty-four. But despite His years, He wished to set out as quickly as possible for Europe and America to proclaim His Father's Faith. In September 1910 He left for Egypt, intending to travel to Europe from there. His health was so poor, however, that He was obliged to stay there for almost a year.

He finally arrived in Europe in August 1911. Although He was totally unfamiliar with Western customs and languages and had never before spoken in public, He gave dozens of talks everywhere and spoke to hundreds of people of many races and creeds. Indefatigably, the almost seventy-year-old 'Abdu'l-Bahá travelled from country to country for two whole years. Beginning in France, He travelled to England, then back to France and afterwards to Egypt, from where He set out for America. There, He

'Abdu'l-Bahá in America . . .

. . . *and in Germany*

visited thirty-eight cities in eight months. Everywhere He went He made such a great impression on His audience that many believed He himself was the Manifestation of God, the Return of Christ. In December 1912 He left the United States and once more travelled to Britain and France, then to Germany, Hungary and Austria. From Vienna He returned via Germany and France to Egypt. Finally, in December 1913, He arrived back in the Holy

Land, completely exhausted from so many tiring journeys.

His efforts had been wonderfully successful. Wherever He had spoken, groups of Bahá'ís had been formed who began enthusiastically carrying on His work. Only in Persia (now Iran) was the situation as bad as ever. Bahá'ís continued to be tortured and put to death. And yet the number of believers continued to grow. To such an extent, in fact, that today there are about half a million Iranian Bahá'ís spread all over the world.

But let us return to 'Abdu'l-Bahá, who was receiving large numbers of visitors daily in His home in Haifa. Suddenly, in February 1914, 'Abdu'l-Bahá began sending His visitors back to their homelands and refusing to receive any more. No one could understand this. 'Abdu'l-Bahá knew that soon a great war would break out, making it impossible for the pilgrims to return to their own countries. Six months later the Great War in fact broke out – just as Bahá'u'lláh had prophesied to the kings and rulers of His time. Once again 'Abdu'l-Bahá was prevented from leaving the city and the Turkish commander threatened that He would be crucified. For two years, 'Abdu'l-Bahá had to live with this threat, conscious that each day could be His last. When the British finally took Haifa on 23 September 1918, there was general rejoicing when it was found that 'Abdu'l-Bahá was safe.

From then onwards 'Abdu'l-Bahá was again occupied in answering the enormous number of letters which He received from many countries. He still carried on His work of visiting the poor and the sick, caring for them and giving them money. In the evenings He usually received visitors and told them amusing stories or explained the Bahá'í teachings to them. For three years He guided the world Bahá'í community in this way.

On 28 November 1921 'Abdu'l-Bahá passed away at the age of seventy-seven after a short illness. The following day ten thousand people of every rank and of many different religions, races and nationalities, attended the funeral and mourned the loss of their beloved Master. He was laid to rest, as He had wished, in one of the rooms of the Shrine of the Báb.

13

The formative age

The passing of 'Abdu'l-Bahá in 1921 marked the beginning of a new phase in the history of the Bahá'í Faith. The age in which its three major figures (the Báb, Bahá'u'lláh and 'Abdu'l-Bahá) had lived was now past. This heroic age, in which twenty thousand believers were put to death for their faith in the Báb and Bahá'u'lláh, the twin Manifestations of God for this day, had come to an end. But if you consider how far the Bahá'í Faith has spread around the world since 1921, you will see that they did not sacrifice their lives in vain.

During the lifetime of Bahá'u'lláh, the number of countries in which His followers lived was still quite small. Between 1853 and 1892 their number had only increased from two to fifteen. This was mainly because Bahá'u'lláh was a prisoner right up to the end of His life and not allowed to travel. Even after His passing, the spread of the Faith was hampered, since His successor, 'Abdu'l-Bahá, was for a long time not allowed to leave the country either. It was only after His release in 1908 that He began the teaching work proper. His journeys to Europe and America, in particular, resulted in a rapid increase in the number of believers. By the end of His life, the number of countries where Bahá'ís lived had increased to thirty-seven.

It was naturally very important at that time that there should be someone to take over the direction of the Bahá'í community. In His Will and Testament, 'Abdu'l-Bahá had appointed His eldest grandson to this task. This was Shoghi Effendi, who, at the age of only twenty-four, suddenly found himself appointed Guardian of the Faith. It was his task to maintain unity amongst the believers and to ensure that no discord should arise. In addition, he was now responsible for the further spread of the Bahá'í teachings worldwide. But he also had another task.

For the first time a Manifestation of God had given detailed instructions for the organisation of His religion. Bahá'u'lláh had done this because after the passing of earlier Manifestations there had always been difficulties about how things should be organised. There were never any precise instructions to the followers of previous religions and so they never knew which was the best way to work together. This problem had been solved by Bahá'u'lláh and 'Abdu'l-Bahá. The organisational structure had been laid down. It was now Shoghi Effendi's task to put it into effect.

This was no easy job, but it was necessary, since so much teaching work had still to be done. To do this properly, it was not enough for each Bahá'í to do his bit nor for everyone to be doing the same thing. The work had to be shared, and for this guidance was needed. Besides, it was vital to maintain the unity of the Bahá'í community; otherwise it, too, might well split up into groups, each with their own ideas. Then, just as in the other religions, there would be disunity which would cause a great deal of trouble. Therefore 'Abdu'l-Bahá had appointed the Guardian to be the sole interpreter of the Words of Bahá'u'lláh and 'Abdu'l-Bahá.

Let us now take a look at this organisational structure. Bahá'u'lláh has laid down that in every locality where nine or more Bahá'ís reside, an assembly must be formed or elected. The assembly, which has nine members, is responsible for organising the work of the Faith in that locality and is therefore called the Local Spiritual Assembly. When there is a sufficient number of local assemblies in a country, a National Spiritual Assembly is elected by the Bahá'ís of that country to administer the work of the Faith there. In addition, the assemblies may also appoint committees to assist them in their work, since if large numbers of Bahá'ís reside in one country or city, the

A National Spiritual Assembly in Africa

assembly will not be able to cope with all the work itself. There may, for example, be book-publishing committees, youth committees, summer school or teaching committees.

The Bahá'í Faith has no clergy. On the contrary, every Bahá'í is called upon to help in the organisation and spread of the Faith. All Bahá'ís have equal rights and any believer over 21 is eligible for election to an assembly. People younger than this can serve as members of committees. No one is superior or inferior. All Bahá'ís, however, must accept the decisions of the assembly. For if everyone followed his or her own inclinations, the result would, of course, be chaotic. That is why organisation is needed. And it must run smoothly or it will not work at all.

Let us return for a moment to Shoghi Effendi, who had to set up the whole organisation. You will realise that he could not do it alone. He needed the cooperation of all the followers of Bahá'u'lláh. And this he received. Many of

Members of assemblies consulting together

them were filled with such enthusiasm that, one after another, they left their countries to spread the teachings abroad. The majority nevertheless stayed at home, since there was so much to be done in their own countries.

Apart from the ongoing persecution in Persia and other Islamic countries, the situation of the believers in Russia was very difficult after the Communist revolution of 1917. Some five hundred of them were taken prisoner and many were sent to Siberia. The rest were obliged to return to Persia since the Communists would have nothing to do with religion. Likewise, in Nazi Germany all Bahá'í activities were forbidden in the period just before World War II.

Nevertheless, the devoted efforts of the Bahá'ís all over the world brought great victories for the Faith. In twenty years the number of countries in which Bahá'ís resided increased to over seventy. And in 1926 the first person of royal blood became a Bahá'í. This was Queen Marie of Romania who was convinced that the teachings of Bahá'u'lláh were the only solution to the world's problems. However, since she was the only monarch who held this opinion, whilst the others all thought they themselves knew best, world war broke out once more. Just as 'Abdu'l-Bahá had prophesied after the end of the First World War. 'Another war,' He said, 'fiercer than the last, will assuredly break out.' And when it did, it greatly restricted Bahá'í activities except in the USA and Latin America. In fulfilment of 'Abdu'l-Bahá's 'Divine Plan', Shoghi Effendi began a series of plans in 1937 and when the war was over the believers were able to continue the teaching work. For the first time all the

Shoghi Effendi
Guardian of the
Bahá'í Faith

National Assemblies then in existence had definite plans for spreading the Faith. These were followed by a global ten-year plan, launched by Shoghi Effendi in 1953. The goal of this 'Ten Year Crusade' was to involve the Bahá'ís all over the world in taking the Message of Bahá'u'lláh to the remaining countries in which as yet no Bahá'í resided. The result was tremendous. Whereas in 1953 there had been only twelve National Assemblies, by 1963 there were fifty-six. Likewise, the number of local assemblies increased enormously. In 1953 there had been 611; ten years later, in 1963, the number was 3,552. In 1953 Bahá'ís resided in only 2,425 localities in the world; by 1963 this number had increased to 11,000.

The Guardian, alas, did not live to see the brilliant results of his plan. He passed away suddenly in London, where he had been on a visit, on 4 November 1957. What did come about during his lifetime, however, was the recognition of the Bahá'í International Community by the United Nations. This took place in 1947 when the Bahá'ís were admitted as observers, and when later they were given consultative status the Bahá'í delegation was able to make numerous proposals and contributions to the subjects being discussed.

During the Guardian's lifetime, too, the dedication took place in 1953 of the first Bahá'í House of Worship in the West, a magnificent building on the shores of Lake Michigan in the United States, which had taken over forty years to complete. Later Houses of Worship were built in every continent of the world: in Frankfurt for Europe, in Kampala for Africa, in Sydney for Australasia, in Panama for South America, in Samoa for the Pacific, and most recently in New Delhi for Asia.

In the same period the Shrines of Bahá'u'lláh and the Báb in the Holy Land, holiest places of pilgrimage to Bahá'ís around the world, were made even more beautiful. Near the Shrine of the Báb on Mount Carmel began to grow the world spiritual and administrative centre of the Bahá'í Faith, surrounded by gardens (see photographs).

Let us continue with the year 1963. As we saw, the Bahá'í community had grown enormously. The time was now ripe for the election of an international assembly which would direct Bahá'í activities worldwide. After all, there were now National Assemblies in fifty-six countries. In 1963, therefore, the first international assembly of nine people was elected. To this assembly was given, as prescribed by Bahá'u'lláh, the name of Universal House of Justice. From then on, this body was responsible for directing the affairs of the Faith and all the believers were subject to its decisions.

The Bahá'í World Centre, 1984. Left to right: The Seat of the Universal House of Justice, the Archives Building, the Shrine of the Báb

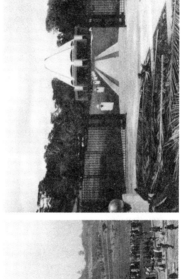

Bahá'í Houses of Worship.
Opposite page, clockwise from top:
Wilmette, Illinois, USA;
Frankfurt, Federal Republic of Germany;
Kampala, Uganda; Sydney, Australia.
This page: Panama; Apia, Samoa;
New Delhi, India.

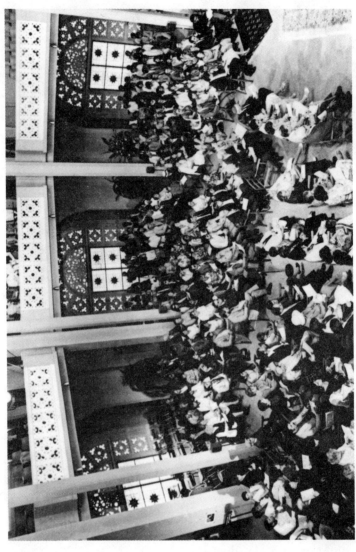

Inside the Bahá'í House of Worship in Sydney. Each House of Worship has nine doors, opening into one central hall and symbolising the unity of peoples from different backgrounds

Just as the Guardian had done, the Universal House of Justice drew up plans for the further spread of the Bahá'í Faith. In 1967, for example, 140 world leaders received a booklet containing the letters written by Bahá'u'lláh a hundred years earlier to the rulers of His day. A nine-year plan had also been drawn up in 1964, the results of which were again momentous. During this period the number of National Assemblies was raised from 69 to 113, of Local Assemblies from 4,566 to 5,902 and the number of localities where Bahá'ís resided, from 15,186 to 31,883. Immediately afterwards, in 1974, a five-year plan was launched. This raised the number of National Assemblies to 125, the number of Local Assemblies to approximately 20,000 and the number of localities where Bahá'ís resided to about 102,000, by 1979.

In that same year, however, another terrible event took place in Iran. In February a revolution broke out which forced the Shah to flee the country and brought the religious leader, the Ayatollah Khomeini, to power. Since Khomeini wished to found a purely Islamic state, he began again the persecution of all the Bahá'ís living in Iran. During the last few years, therefore, hundreds of Bahá'ís have been imprisoned and at least two hundred have been executed, some after having been tortured. Thousands of houses have been raided and burned to the ground, leaving over ten thousand Bahá'ís homeless.

All these terrorist activities however, have achieved the opposite of what Khomeini wished. The Faith has spread. And how did this happen? All over the world, newspaper and television reports have highlighted the persecution of

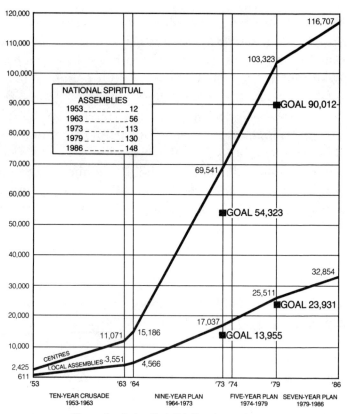

Growth of the Bahá'í Faith 1953–1986

the Bahá'ís in Iran and made the Bahá'í Faith better known than ever. Within seven years, by 1986, there were 148 National Assemblies, 32,854 Local Assemblies and 116,707 localities in which Bahá'ís resided. If you put all these figures together in the form of a graph, you will see that the number of Bahá'u'lláh's followers increases every year.

And then, at the end of 1985, the Universal House of Justice issued a statement addressed for the first time in its history to the peoples of the world, on the occasion of the 1986 International Year of Peace. Entitled *The Promise of World Peace*, this statement sets forth the Bahá'í teachings on peace and how to achieve it, as well as the obstacles to be overcome. It was presented to 167 world leaders by early in 1986, and then began its long journey to reach the heart of every person on the planet. So far it has been translated into 47 languages and published in 143 editions, and is helping people all over the world in their efforts to understand what peace really means, and what we have to do to get it. For everyone wants to live in peace.

Before closing this section, let us go back once again to the time in which Bahá'u'lláh lived. Over one hundred and twenty years ago He prophesied that the time would come in which everyone would follow Him. Although that time is a long way off, the Bahá'ís are firmly convinced – and with reason – that Bahá'u'lláh spoke the truth. For in spite of all attempts, past and present, to exterminate their Faith, every day people all over the world declare their belief in Bahá'u'lláh. People who are convinced that only the teachings of the latest Manifestation of God, Bahá'u'lláh, can really help us to overcome our problems and show us the way to happiness and peace.

IV

THE FOLLOWERS OF BAHÁ'U'LLÁH

14

What does it mean to be a Bahá'í?

To answer this question, we first need to establish what a Bahá'í is and is not. A Bahá'í is definitely not a saint. And not someone whose spiritual qualities are all developed to the full. No, first and foremost a Bahá'í is an ordinary human being just like everyone else. The only difference is that a Bahá'í is a follower of Bahá'u'lláh and therefore accepts Bahá'u'lláh as his or her divine Teacher. A Bahá'í should therefore be regarded as a student of Bahá'u'lláh and not someone who knows everything and can do anything. Because this is certainly not the case.

To be a Bahá'í means two things, therefore. Firstly, it means that with Bahá'u'lláh's help you are working on the development of your divine qualities and capacities. And secondly it means that you are working for the unity of mankind in the way taught by Bahá'u'lláh.

Let us begin with the development of your divine qualities, also called spiritual growth. I have repeatedly referred to the help we receive from Bahá'u'lláh Himself in doing this. The question is now what is this help and how do you receive it? To explain this, I shall tell you something else first. Imagine that you want to dig the garden. What you need for this is not only a spade but also the will to do it. Let us say you have the will. So what do you do? You begin to dig. At the end of half an hour you are exhausted. Your stomach is rumbling, you have eaten nothing and you have not the strength to finish the job. Food is therefore necessary to do physical work. No matter how much you want to dig the garden, you will not get far if you do not eat something. This is obvious.

The case is exactly the same if you want to develop spiritual qualities. What you need for this is not only the capacity but also the will to develop them. Well, you already have the capacity in yourself. Let us say you also have the will. So what do you do? You begin to develop these capacities. At the end of a week, or even a few days, you are exhausted. You have become mentally tired and have not the strength to go on. What you need is fresh spiritual strength, fresh spiritual food. This spiritual food is necessary for spiritual work and for spiritual growth. Just as material food is necessary for physical work or necessary for a child to grow physically. You may well have a great desire to grow spiritually but if you have no spiritual food you will not get far.

It is therefore important to know how to obtain this spiritual food and spiritual strength. Well, as you know, the source of this spiritual strength is the Manifestation of God Himself. If you want to receive this strength you must turn to Him. You must turn your thoughts to Bahá'u'lláh and ask Him for this strength. This is what we call prayer. It is quite different from just reciting a few sentences without thinking much about what you are saying. In the first place, you must turn to Bahá'u'lláh. When you have done this, you say slowly one of the prayers which He has given us specially for this purpose. Then you reflect on what you have just read. Only then will you receive the spiritual strength you need for your spiritual growth, for the development of your divine qualities. Only then can you really achieve the purpose of your life.

Blessed is the spot,
and the house,
and the place,
and the city,
and the heart,
and the mountain,
and the refuge,
and the cave,
and the valley,
and the land,
and the sea,
and the island,
and the meadow
where mention of God
hath been made,
and His praise glorified.

Bahá'u'lláh

So being a Bahá'í means that you take spiritual food every day. You do this by reading some of the writings of your divine Teacher, Bahá'u'lláh, every morning and every evening. You do not have to read pages and pages. If you only read a few sentences with full concentration, this is enough. In addition, there is one special prayer you say every day.

If you do this, you will notice how much faster your spiritual qualities develop than if you do not do it. This is not a fairy tale, but a fact. Every Bahá'í has found this out by personal experience. At first it may take some effort to get started, but if you learn gradually to make a habit of it, then eventually you will not want to miss a single day. Because you will have discovered that you can have contact with Bahá'u'lláh and have experienced how wonderful it is to be in touch with your divine Teacher. And you soon notice that your divine qualities are developing faster than ever. And that means that you are on your way to becoming a person who loves humanity and tries to serve mankind and work for world peace. You are on your way to becoming a worthwhile, kind and happy person.

Secondly, to be a Bahá'í means that you are working for the unity of mankind. This probably sounds a little vague to you. So we will take a look at exactly what this means.

As you know, the Bahá'ís do not place much confidence in the short-term remedy or what we called earlier the 'stomach tablet'. This means that, for Bahá'ís, it does not make much sense to confine ourselves to writing letters to political prisoners, for example, or giving money to the Third World. This will not really solve the problems. Of course, the prisoner of conscience is glad to have a letter and the hungry child to get some food, but the effects of this kind of help are short-lived. In a short time the prisoner feels sad again and the child is hungry. And, in addition, there will still be political prisoners and undernourished children.

This is why the Bahá'ís are assisting people to achieve their own economic and social development. Poor people, hungry people, need help to develop their own resources so that they can rebuild their lives on a sure foundation. That is why Bahá'ís throughout the world – the Third World *and* the 'developed' world – are carrying out social and economic development projects for their communities, starting from the grass-roots. These projects can be the setting up of schools, centres for primary health care, farming or rural development, help for homeless people, help for people addicted to drugs or alcohol, projects to assist women achieve their equality, and many more.

Bahá'ís are concerned with the causes of the problems. Only when the causes are known and removed can the problems really be solved. This is why Bahá'ís do their best to pass on the Message of Bahá'u'lláh to other people. After all, this Message tells us what are the causes of the problems and also how we can remove them.

This does not mean that Bahá'ís go from door to door or stand on street corners handing out pamphlets, although sometimes this is done. But it is very important, too, for Bahá'ís to become friendly with other people. Because it is only when Bahá'ís show by their deeds that they can make others a little happier that people become interested in

Rural development at the Dorothy Baker Centre for Environmental Education, Cochabamba, Bolivia

Ploughing with a team of water-buffalo used in addition to a tractor at the Rabbani School, India

Making the best of stony ground; a nursery for seedlings in Liancourt, Haiti

Primary health care in Kenya: a community health worker receives her diploma

A class in nutrition at Nakuru

Looking at germs: a training course at the Menu Bahá'í Institute

A literacy class for tribal women in India

'Radio Bahá'í' announcer in Panama, a member of the Guaymi people

A nursery school at Khlatakulu, Swaziland

Italy: National Bahá'í Youth Symposium

India: Laying the cornerstone at the site of the Bahá'í Youth Academy in Maharashtra

them and in what they believe. It is only when you like a person that you want to know what his interests are, what he does in his daily life and what he thinks about life in general. Words alone are no use. People want first to see deeds. Then they will be interested in words and in the Message of Bahá'u'lláh.

So Bahá'ís do not merely use beautiful words to teach their faith; they also teach by means of good deeds and by their daily lives. Once they have found someone who is interested in hearing what they believe in, they will naturally sit down with that person and tell him or her about the Bahá'í Faith.

As soon as a Bahá'í is twenty-one years of age, he or she is eligible for election to a Local or National Spiritual Assembly. As a member of an assembly he or she will be concerned with the organisation of all kinds of activities. A Bahá'í may also be asked to serve on one of the many committees which have various functions such as organising teaching activities or study classes, youth activities, summer schools and so on. It does not matter what one does as long as it helps the spread of the Faith. Some people do this by writing books, others by holding 'fireside' meetings and yet others give public talks. There are a thousand and one ways. Each Bahá'í is free to choose to give a hand where he can best do so, whether in preparing an exhibition or drawing pictures for children's books. It is important for everyone, man or woman, girl or boy, to do the things they do best. Fortunately, these are different for everyone.

Finally, to be a Bahá'í means that you are part of the Bahá'í world community and that together we are all working for the unity of the human race. Working together is of course essential. If you try to do it all by yourself you will get nowhere. After all, there are about 4,500 million people in the world and you are only one of them. If we want to achieve anything, it is essential to work as a community. In addition to this, it is equally important for the community to keep growing in size, which means in strength as well. The larger the community, the more it will be listened to. The larger the community, the more work it can do. The larger the community, the more influence it will have. You notice this everywhere. The larger organisations are, the more they can achieve. The larger a political party is, the more say it has. If you are on your own and make a plea to stop the hunting of seals, for example, no one will take much notice. Only if you join with others, thus becoming stronger, will you be listened to. This is obvious.

So if you are a Bahá'í, you work with the community. The way this works is that every Bahá'í – whether six or sixty years old – has the opportunity of putting forward ideas or suggestions; for example, for making the Faith known in his or her district. These and other suggestions will be considered by the Assembly and, if they are approved, then they can be carried out. Many Bahá'ís have the chance to serve on a committee. It is a privilege to be asked to serve in this way but of course if you find it is not possible to do so, you can be excused. And, as you know, once you reach the age of twenty-one, you may be elected to serve on an assembly.

Apart from these activities, Bahá'ís meet regularly for other reasons. Some of these may be to get to know each other better, to help each other with the work they are doing, to study a particular subject together or just to be sociable. However, they will all meet every nineteen days at what is called the Nineteen Day Feast. The Bahá'í year also has nine Holy Days on which work is suspended. Some of these are days of celebration, such as the Bahá'í New Year (on 21 March), the Declaration of Bahá'u'lláh, His birthday and that of the Báb. Others are commemoration days.

In addition to these Holy Days there are numerous other meetings. The youth may have regular weekend meetings, camps or conferences. And there are the summer and winter schools with lectures and classes for every age group. You are not obliged to attend these meetings but of course you are very welcome. The important thing is that if you want to take an active part in the Bahá'í community, you will have every opportunity to do so.

15

How do you become a Bahá'í?

By now it will be clear that to be a Bahá'í you do not need to be a saint. If you were one, it would be quite unnecessary to become a Bahá'í. You would already have developed all your spiritual qualities to the full and the purpose of your life would have been fulfilled. On the contrary, you do not even have to have developed any qualities at all. The only thing needed is that you are prepared to start. Even if you were a criminal, as long as you had the will to develop your spiritual capacities, you could become a Bahá'í.

However, there is more to it than this. You must, of course, believe in God. Then you must recognise Bahá'u'lláh as the Messenger of God for this Age. In doing so you will naturally accept His teachings and laws. Finally, you must be prepared to accept what is called the Bahá'í Administrative Order. This includes the assemblies, local and national, and, above all, the Universal House of Justice, the highest authority in the Faith.

As soon as you think all this applies to you, you can ask for a card on which you will find these requirements mentioned once again. All you have to do then is sign this card. In doing so, you are declaring yourself to be a Bahá'í and you are then a follower of Bahá'u'lláh. You need not be afraid you will have to undergo any kind of ritual or ceremony. Your signature is sufficient. After all, it is a matter between you and your Creator whether you wish to become a follower of His Manifestation for this age. Then, when your National Assembly registers your name, you become a member of the Bahá'í community. Of course this does not mean the other Bahá'ís will leave you to your own resources. On the contrary, they will do their best to make you feel at home in the community and help you along your future path.

The only thing left to tell you is that Bahá'ís recognise the age of fifteen as the age of spiritual responsibility. Up to that age a person is in the spiritual care of his or her parents. This means that if you are less than fifteen years old when you want to become a Bahá'í you should ask your parents for their approval first.

When you become a Bahá'í, you will be joining in the most exciting and worthwhile activity that can be imagined today. You will be working for the most important cause in existence, namely the cause of world peace. You will be helping to achieve the age-old dream of a world where people live in peace and unity and where the earth is really seen to be 'but one country'.

Suggestions for further reading

There are more than 500 books about the Bahá'í Faith published in English, so this is a very partial list.

The Sacred Texts of the Bahá'í Faith include all the Writings of Bahá'u'lláh, the Báb and 'Abdu'l-Bahá. From the Writings of Bahá'u'lláh, *The Hidden Words* is perhaps the best to begin with. *Paris Talks* by 'Abdu'l-Bahá will give you an idea of the teachings of the Bahá'í Faith.

A classic outline is *Bahá'u'lláh and the New Era* by J. E. Esslemont, which includes many quotations from the Sacred Texts. All these books are published in several countries, including the UK, USA and India. Some other suggestions are:

Call to the Nations. A selection of Shoghi Effendi's writings. Haifa: Bahá'í World Centre, 1977.

The Promise of World Peace. The 'Peace Message' of the Universal House of Justice issued in 1985. Several editions, including an illustrated one (Oneworld Publications, London) and a video.

Prayers and Thoughts for Peace. A pocket-size edition. London: Bahá'í Publishing Trust, 1986.

Ali's Dream: The Story of Bahá'u'lláh. John Hatcher. Oxford: George Ronald, 1980.

Hour of the Dawn: The Life of the Báb. Mary Perkins. Oxford: George Ronald, 1987.

Vignettes from the Life of 'Abdu'l-Bahá. Annamarie Honnold. Oxford: George Ronald, 1982.

Unrestrained as the Wind. Selections from the Sacred Text and the Universal House of Justice about distinctive Bahá'í qualities and actions. Bahá'í National Youth Committee of the United States. Wilmette: Bahá'í Publishing Trust, 1985.

The publisher acknowledges with gratitude permission to print the illustrations appearing on the pages listed below: Bahá'í World Centre, pp. 63, 88, 94, 112, 113, 116, 121, 122, 126, 129, 134, 135, 137, 139, 140, 141, 142, 146, 152, 158; International Labour Office, pp. 46, 51, 52; World Council of Churches, p. 23; United Nations Organization, p. 22 (UN photo 148893), p. 41 (UN photo 134160), p. 45 (UN photo 149447), p. 57 (UN photo 139209). Len Sirman Press, pp. 2, 67; Amedé Chatriand, pp. 12, 36, 102, 151; Audrey Marcus, Hugh Chance and Eunice Braun, pp. 107, 110, 115; David Ruhe, pp. 118, 131; Paul Slaughter, p. 141 (House of Worship in New Delhi); Ethel Martens, pp. 156, 157; Hassan Sabri, pp. 155, 157; Mahmoud Samandari, p. 72; Lian Bates, the idea on p. 24.